Cliffs Quick Review

Accounting Principles I

by
Elizabeth A. Minbiole, CPA MBA

About the Author:
Elizabeth A. Minbiole, CPA MBA

Acknowledgment:
I would like to thank Richard Guittar for his help with this book. He edited and typeset the manuscript, produced the illustrations, and cowrote significant portions of the text.

Dedication:
To Mark and Thomas, whose love and understanding have helped make this book possible.

Cover Photograph
GSO Images / The Image Bank

Production
Wiley Indianapolis Composition Services

CliffsQuickReview™ *Accounting Principles I*

Published by:
Learneo, Inc.

CONTENTS

CONTENTS

CONTENTS

CONTENTS

CONTENTS

Accounting is the language of business. It is the system of recording, summarizing, and analyzing an economic entity's financial transactions. Effectively communicating this information is key to the success of every business. Those who rely on financial information include internal users, such as a company's managers and employees, and external users, such as banks, investors, governmental agencies, financial analysts, and labor unions. These users depend upon data supplied by accountants to answer the following types of questions:

- Is the company profitable?
- Is there enough cash to meet payroll needs?
- How much debt does the company have?
- How does the company's net income compare to its budget?
- What is the balance owed by customers?
- Has the company consistently paid cash dividends?
- How much income does each division generate?
- Should the company invest money to expand?

Accountants must present an organization's financial information in clear, concise reports that help make questions like these easy to answer. The most common accounting reports are called financial statements.

Financial Statements

The financial statements shown on the next several pages are for a **sole proprietorship,** which is a business owned by an individual. Corporate financial statements are slightly different. The four basic financial statements are the income statement, statement of owner's equity, balance sheet, and statement of cash flows. The income statement, statement of owner's equity, and statement of cash flows report activity for a specific period of time, usually a month, quarter, or year. The balance sheet reports balances of certain elements at a specific time. All four statements have a three-line heading in the following format:

Name of Company
Name of Statement
Time Period or Date

Income statement. The **income statement,** which is sometimes called the statement of earnings or statement of operations, is prepared first. It lists revenues and expenses and calculates the company's net income or net loss for a period of time. **Net income** means total revenues are greater than total expenses. **Net loss** means total expenses are greater than total revenues. The specific items that appear in financial statements are explained later.

The Greener Landscape Group
Income Statement
For the Month Ended April 30, 20X2

Revenues		
Lawn Cutting Revenue		$845
Expenses		
Wages Expense	$280	
Depreciation Expense	235	
Insurance Expense	100	
Interest Expense	79	
Advertising Expense	35	
Gas Expense	30	
Supplies Expense	25	
Total Expenses		784
Net Income		$ 61

Statement of owner's equity. The statement of owner's equity is prepared after the income statement. It shows the beginning and ending owner's equity balances and the items affecting owner's equity during the period. These items include investments, the net income or loss from the income statement, and withdrawals. Because the specific revenue and expense categories that determine net income or loss appear on the income statement, the statement of owner's equity shows only the total net income or loss. Balances enclosed by parentheses are subtracted from unenclosed balances.

The Greener Landscape Group
Statement of Owner's Equity
For the Month Ended April 30, 20X2

J. Green, Capital, April 1		$ 0
Additions		
Investments	$15,000	
Net Income	61	15,061
Withdrawals		(50)
J. Green, Capital, April 30		$15,011

Balance sheet. The balance sheet shows the balance, at a particular time, of each asset, each liability, and owner's equity. It proves that the **accounting equation** (Assets = Liabilities + Owner's Equity) is in balance. The ending balance on the statement of owner's equity is used to report owner's equity on the balance sheet.

The Greener Landscape Group
Balance Sheet
April 30, 20X2

ASSETS			
Current Assets			
Cash			$ 6,355
Accounts Receivable			200
Supplies			25
Prepaid Insurance			1,100
Total Current Assets			7,680
Property, Plant, and Equipment			
Equipment		$18,000	
Less: Accumulated Depreciation		(235)	17,765
Total Assets			$25,445
LIABILITIES AND OWNER'S EQUITY			
Current Liabilities			
Accounts Payable			$ 50
Wages Payable			80
Interest Payable			79
Unearned Revenue			225
Total Current Liabilities			434
Long-Term Liabilities			
Notes Payable			10,000
Total Liabilities			10,434
Owner's Equity			
J. Green, Capital			15,011
Total Liabilities and Owner's Equity			$25,445

Statement of cash flows. The statement of cash flows tracks the movement of cash during a specific accounting period. It assigns all cash exchanges to one of three categories—operating, investing, or financing—to calculate the net change in cash and then reconciles the accounting period's beginning and ending cash balances. As its name implies, the statement of cash flows includes items that affect cash. Although not part of the statement's main body, significant non-cash items must also be disclosed.

According to current accounting standards, operating cash flows may be disclosed using either the direct or the indirect method. The direct method simply lists the net cash flow by type of cash receipt and payment category. The indirect method is explained in *Cliffs Quick Review Accounting Principles II*. For purposes of illustration, the direct method appears below.

The Greener Landscape Group
Statement of Cash Flows
For the Month Ended April 30, 20X2

Cash Flows from Operating Activities	
Cash from Customers	$ 870
Cash to Employees	(200)
Cash to Suppliers	(1,265)
Cash Flow Used by Operating Activities	(595)
Cash Flows from Investing Activities	
Purchases of Equipment	(8,000)
Cash Flows from Financing Activities	
Investment by Owner	15,000
Withdrawal by Owner	(50)
Cash Flow Provided by Financing Activities	14,950
Net Increase in Cash	6,355
Beginning Cash, April 1	0
Ending Cash, April 30	$ 6,355

Noncash Financing and Investing Activity
The company purchased a used truck for $15,000, paying $5,000 in cash and signing a note for the remaining balance. The note payable portion of the transaction is not included on this statement.

The Accounting Equation

The ability to read financial statements requires an understanding of
the items they include and the standard categories used to classify
these items. The accounting equation identifies the relationship between the elements of accounting.

$$\boxed{\text{Assets}} = \boxed{\text{Liabilities}} + \boxed{\begin{array}{c}\text{Owner's}\\\text{Equity}\end{array}}$$

Assets. An **asset** is something of value the company owns. Assets
can be tangible or intangible. **Tangible assets** are generally divided
into three major categories: current assets (including cash, marketable
securities, accounts receivable, inventory, and prepaid expenses); property, plant, and equipment; and long-term investments. **Intangible
assets** lack physical substance, but they may, nevertheless, provide
substantial value to the company that owns them. Examples of intangible assets include patents, copyrights, trademarks, and franchise
licenses. A brief description of some tangible assets follows.

- **Current assets** typically include cash and assets the company
  reasonably expects to use, sell, or collect within one year. Current assets appear on the balance sheet (and in the numbered
  list below) in order, from most liquid to least liquid. **Liquid
  assets** are readily convertible into cash or other assets, and
  they are generally accepted as payment for liabilities.

  1. **Cash** includes cash on hand (petty cash), bank balances
     (checking, savings, or money-market accounts), and cash
     equivalents. **Cash equivalents** are highly liquid investments,
     such as certificates of deposit and U.S. treasury bills, with
     maturities of ninety days or less at the time of purchase.

  2. **Marketable securities** include short-term investments in
     stocks, bonds (debt), certificates of deposit, or other securities.
     These items are classified as marketable securities—rather
     than long-term investments—only if the company has both
     the ability and the desire to sell them within one year.

3. **Accounts receivable** are amounts owed to the company by customers who have received products or services but have not yet paid for them.

4. **Inventory** is the cost to acquire or manufacture merchandise for sale to customers. Although service enterprises that never provide customers with merchandise do not use this category for current assets, inventory usually represents a significant portion of assets in merchandising and manufacturing companies.

5. **Prepaid expenses** are amounts paid by the company to purchase items or services that represent future costs of doing business. Examples include office supplies, insurance premiums, and advance payments for rent. These assets become expenses as they expire or get used up.

- **Property, plant, and equipment** is the title given to long-lived assets the business uses to help generate revenue. This category is sometimes called fixed assets. Examples include land, natural resources such as timber or mineral reserves, buildings, production equipment, vehicles, and office furniture. With the exception of land, the cost of an asset in this category is allocated to expense over the asset's estimated useful life.

- **Long-term investments** include purchases of debt or stock issued by other companies and investments with other companies in joint ventures. Long-term investments differ from marketable securities because the company intends to hold long-term investments for more than one year or the securities are not marketable.

Liabilities. **Liabilities** are the company's existing debts and obligations owed to third parties. Examples include amounts owed to suppliers for goods or services received (accounts payable), to employees for work performed (wages payable), and to banks for principal and interest on loans (notes payable and interest payable). Liabilities are generally classified as short-term (current) if they are due in one year or less. Long-term liabilities are not due for at least one year.

Owner's equity. Owner's equity represents the amount owed to the owner or owners by the company. Algebraically, this amount is calculated by subtracting liabilities from each side of the accounting equation. Owner's equity also represents the **net assets** of the company.

$$\boxed{\text{Assets}} - \boxed{\text{Liabilities}} = \boxed{\begin{array}{c}\text{Owner's}\\\text{Equity}\end{array}} = \boxed{\begin{array}{c}\text{Net}\\\text{Assets}\end{array}}$$

In a sole proprietorship or partnership, owner's equity equals the total net investment in the business plus the net income or loss generated during the business's life. **Net investment** equals the sum of all investment in the business by the owner or owners minus withdrawals made by the owner or owners. The owner's investment is recorded in the owner's capital account, and any withdrawals are recorded in a separate owner's drawing account. For example, if a business owner contributes $10,000 to start a company but later withdraws $1,000 for personal expenses, the owner's net investment equals $9,000. **Net income** or **net loss** equals the company's revenues less its expenses. **Revenues** are inflows of money or other assets received from customers in exchange for goods or services. **Expenses** are the costs incurred to generate those revenues.

Components of Owner's Equity in a Sole Proprietorship

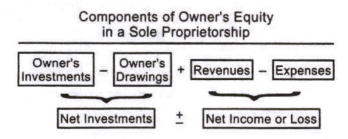

Capital investments and revenues increase owner's equity, while expenses and owner withdrawals (drawings) decrease owner's equity. In a partnership, there are separate capital and drawing accounts for each partner.

Stockholders' equity. In a corporation, ownership is represented by shares of stock, so the owners' equity is called **stockholders' equity** or **shareholders' equity.** Corporations use several types of accounts to record stockholders' equity activities: preferred stock, common stock, paid-in capital (these are often referred to as contributed capital), and retained earnings. **Contributed capital** accounts record the total amount invested by stockholders in the corporation. If a corporation issues more than one class of stock, separate accounts are maintained for each class. **Retained earnings** equal net income or loss over the life of the business less any amounts given back to stockholders in the form of dividends. Dividends affect stockholders' equity in the same way that owner withdrawals affect owner's equity in sole proprietorships and partnerships.

Components of Stockholders' Equity in a Corporation with Two Classes of Stock

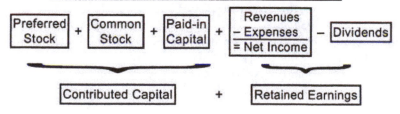

Financial Reporting Objectives

Financial statements are prepared according to agreed upon guidelines. In order to understand these guidelines, it helps to understand the objectives of financial reporting. The objectives of financial reporting, as discussed in the Financial Accounting Standards Board (FASB) *Statement of Financial Accounting Concepts No. 1,* are to provide information that

1. is useful to existing and potential investors and creditors and other users in making rational investment, credit, and similar decisions;

2. helps existing and potential investors and creditors and other users to assess the amounts, timing, and uncertainty of prospective net cash inflows to the enterprise;

3. identifies the economic resources of an enterprise, the claims to those resources, and the effects that transactions, events, and circumstances have on those resources.

Generally Accepted Accounting Principles

Accountants use **generally accepted accounting principles (GAAP)** to guide them in recording and reporting financial information. GAAP comprises a broad set of principles that have been developed by the accounting profession and the Securities and Exchange Commission (SEC). Two laws, the Securities Act of 1933 and the Securities Exchange Act of 1934, give the SEC authority to establish reporting and disclosure requirements. However, the SEC usually operates in an oversight capacity, allowing the FASB and the Governmental Accounting Standards Board (GASB) to establish these requirements. The GASB develops accounting standards for state and local governments.

The current set of principles that accountants use rests upon some underlying assumptions. The basic assumptions and principles presented on the next several pages are considered GAAP and apply to most financial statements. In addition to these concepts, there are other, more technical standards accountants must follow when preparing financial statements. Some of these are discussed later in this book, but others are left for more advanced study.

Economic entity assumption. Financial records must be separately maintained for each economic entity. Economic entities include businesses, governments, school districts, churches, and other social organizations. Although accounting information from many different entities may be combined for financial reporting purposes, every economic event must be associated with and recorded by a specific entity.

In addition, business records must not include the personal assets or liabilities of the owners.

Monetary unit assumption. An economic entity's accounting records include only quantifiable transactions. Certain economic events that affect a company, such as hiring a new chief executive officer or introducing a new product, cannot be easily quantified in monetary units and, therefore, do not appear in the company's accounting records. Furthermore, accounting records must be recorded using a stable currency. Businesses in the United States usually use U.S. dollars for this purpose.

Full disclosure principle. Financial statements normally provide information about a company's past performance. However, pending lawsuits, incomplete transactions, or other conditions may have imminent and significant effects on the company's financial status. The full disclosure principle requires that financial statements include disclosure of such information. Footnotes supplement financial statements to convey this information and to describe the policies the company uses to record and report business transactions.

Time period assumption. Most businesses exist for long periods of time, so artificial time periods must be used to report the results of business activity. Depending on the type of report, the time period may be a day, a month, a year, or another arbitrary period. Using artificial time periods leads to questions about when certain transactions should be recorded. For example, how should an accountant report the cost of equipment expected to last five years? Reporting the entire expense during the year of purchase might make the company seem unprofitable that year and unreasonably profitable in subsequent years. Once the time period has been established, accountants use GAAP to record and report that accounting period's transactions.

Accrual basis accounting. In most cases, GAAP requires the use of accrual basis accounting rather than cash basis accounting. **Accrual basis accounting,** which adheres to the revenue recognition, matching, and cost principles discussed below, captures the financial aspects of each economic event in the accounting period in which it occurs, regardless of when the cash changes hands. Under **cash basis accounting,** revenues are recognized only when the company receives cash or its equivalent, and expenses are recognized only when the company pays with cash or its equivalent.

Revenue recognition principle. Revenue is earned and recognized upon product delivery or service completion, without regard to the timing of cash flow. Suppose a store orders five hundred compact discs from a wholesaler in March, receives them in April, and pays for them in May. The wholesaler recognizes the sales revenue in April when delivery occurs, not in March when the deal is struck or in May when the cash is received. Similarly, if an attorney receives a $100 retainer from a client, the attorney doesn't recognize the money as revenue until he or she actually performs $100 in services for the client.

Matching principle. The costs of doing business are recorded in the same period as the revenue they help to generate. Examples of such costs include the cost of goods sold, salaries and commissions earned, insurance premiums, supplies used, and estimates for potential warranty work on the merchandise sold. Consider the wholesaler who delivered five hundred CDs to a store in April. These CDs change from an asset (inventory) to an expense (cost of goods sold) when the revenue is recognized so that the profit from the sale can be determined.

Cost principle. Assets are recorded at cost, which equals the value exchanged at the time of their acquisition. In the United States, even if assets such as land or buildings appreciate in value over time, they are not revalued for financial reporting purposes.

Going concern principle. Unless otherwise noted, financial statements are prepared under the assumption that the company will remain in business indefinitely. Therefore, assets do not need to be sold at fire-sale values, and debt does not need to be paid off before maturity. This principle results in the classification of assets and liabilities as short-term (current) and long-term. **Long-term assets** are expected to be held for more than one year. **Long-term liabilities** are not due for more than one year.

Relevance, reliability, and consistency. To be useful, financial information must be relevant, reliable, and prepared in a consistent manner. **Relevant information** helps a decision maker understand a company's past performance, present condition, and future outlook so that informed decisions can be made in a timely manner. Of course, the information needs of individual users may differ, requiring that the information be presented in different formats. Internal users often need more detailed information than external users, who may need to know only the company's value or its ability to repay loans. **Reliable information** is verifiable and objective. **Consistent information** is prepared using the same methods each accounting period, which allows meaningful comparisons to be made between different accounting periods and between the financial statements of different companies that use the same methods.

Principle of conservatism. Accountants must use their judgment to record transactions that require estimation. The number of years that equipment will remain productive and the portion of accounts receivable that will never be paid are examples of items that require estimation. In reporting financial data, accountants follow the **principle of conservatism,** which requires that the less optimistic estimate be chosen when two estimates are judged to be equally likely. For example, suppose a manufacturing company's Warranty Repair Department has documented a three-percent return rate for product X during the past two years, but the company's Engineering Department insists this return rate is just a statistical anomaly and less than one percent of product X will require service during the coming year. Unless the Engineering

Department provides compelling evidence to support its estimate, the company's accountant must follow the principle of conservatism and plan for a three-percent return rate. Losses and costs—such as warranty repairs—are recorded when they are probable and reasonably estimated. Gains are recorded when realized.

Materiality principle. Accountants follow the **materiality principle,** which states that the requirements of any accounting principle may be ignored when there is no effect on the users of financial information. Certainly, tracking individual paper clips or pieces of paper is immaterial and excessively burdensome to any company's accounting department. Although there is no definitive measure of materiality, the accountant's judgment on such matters must be sound. Several thousand dollars may not be material to an entity such as General Motors, but that same figure is quite material to a small, family-owned business.

Internal Control

Internal control is the process designed to ensure reliable financial reporting, effective and efficient operations, and compliance with applicable laws and regulations. Safeguarding assets against theft and unauthorized use, acquisition, or disposal is also part of internal control.

Control environment. The management style and the expectations of upper-level managers, particularly their control policies, determine the control environment. An effective **control environment** helps ensure that established policies and procedures are followed. The control environment includes independent oversight provided by a board of directors and, in publicly held companies, by an audit committee; management's integrity, ethical values, and philosophy; a defined organizational structure with competent and trustworthy employees; and the assignment of authority and responsibility.

Control activities. Control activities are the specific policies and procedures management uses to achieve its objectives. The most important control activities involve segregation of duties, proper authorization of transactions and activities, adequate documents and records, physical control over assets and records, and independent checks on performance. A short description of each of these control activities appears below.

- **Segregation of duties** requires that different individuals be assigned responsibility for different elements of related activities, particularly those involving authorization, custody, or recordkeeping. For example, the same person who is responsible for an asset's recordkeeping should not be responsible for physical control of that asset. Having different individuals perform these functions creates a system of checks and balances.

- **Proper authorization** of transactions and activities helps ensure that all company activities adhere to established guidelines unless responsible managers authorize another course of action. For example, a fixed price list may serve as an official authorization of price for a large sales staff. In addition, there may be a control to allow a sales manager to authorize reasonable deviations from the price list.

- **Adequate documents and records** provide evidence that financial statements are accurate. Controls designed to ensure adequate recordkeeping include the creation of invoices and other documents that are easy to use and sufficiently informative; the use of prenumbered, consecutive documents; and the timely preparation of documents.

- **Physical control** over assets and records helps protect the company's assets. These control activities may include electronic or mechanical controls (such as a safe, employee ID cards, fences, cash registers, fireproof files, and locks) or computer-related controls dealing with access privileges or established backup and recovery procedures.

- **Independent checks** on performance, which are carried out by employees who did not do the work being checked, help ensure the reliability of accounting information and the efficiency of operations. For example, a supervisor verifies the accuracy of a retail clerk's cash drawer at the end of the day. Internal auditors may also verify that the supervisor performed the check of the cash drawer.

In order to identify and establish effective controls, management must continually assess the risk, monitor control implementation, and modify controls as needed. Top managers of publicly held companies must sign a statement of responsibility for internal controls and include this statement in their annual report to stockholders.

Analyzing Transactions

The first step in the accounting process is to analyze every transaction (economic event) that affects the business. The accounting equation (Assets = Liabilities + Owner's Equity) must remain in balance after every transaction is recorded, so accountants must analyze each transaction to determine how it affects owner's equity and the different types of assets and liabilities before recording the transaction.

Assume Mr. J. Green invests $15,000 to start a landscape business. This transaction increases the company's assets, specifically cash, by $15,000 and increases owner's equity by $15,000. Notice that the accounting equation remains in balance.

Assets	=	Liabilities	+	Owner's Equity
+ 15,000 (Cash)				+ 15,000 (Owner's Capital)

Mr. Green uses $5,000 of the company's cash to place a down-payment on a used truck that costs $15,000, and he signs a note payable that requires him to pay the remaining $10,000 in eighteen months. This transaction decreases one type of asset (cash) by $5,000, increases another type of asset (vehicles) by $15,000, and increases a liability (notes payable) by $10,000. The accounting equation remains in balance, and Mr. Green now has two types of assets ($10,000 in cash and a vehicle worth $15,000), a liability (a $10,000 note payable), and owner's equity of $15,000.

Assets	=	Liabilities	+	Owner's Equity
+ 15,000 (Cash)				+ 15,000 (Owner's Capital)
− 5,000 (Cash) + 15,000 (Vehicles)		+ 10,000 (Notes Payable)		
25,000	=	10,000	+	15,000

Given the large number of transactions that companies usually have, accountants need a more sophisticated system for recording transactions than the one shown on the previous page. Accountants use the double-entry bookkeeping system to keep the accounting equation in balance and to double-check the numerical accuracy of transaction entries. Under this system, each transaction is recorded using at least two accounts. An **account** is a record of all transactions involving a particular item.

Companies maintain separate accounts for each type of asset (cash, accounts receivable, inventory, etc.), each type of liability (accounts payable, wages payable, notes payable, etc.), owner investments (usually referred to as the owner's capital account in a sole proprietorship), owner drawings (withdrawals made by the owner), each type of revenue (sales revenue, service revenue, etc.), and each type of expense (rent expense, wages expense, etc.). All accounts taken together make up the **general ledger.** For organizational purposes, each account in the general ledger is assigned a number, and companies maintain a **chart of accounts,** which lists the accounts and account numbers.

Account numbers vary significantly from one company to the next, depending on the company's size and complexity. A sole proprietorship may have few accounts, but a multinational corporation may have thousands of accounts and use ten- or even twenty-digit numbers to track accounts by location, department, project code, and other categories. Most companies numerically separate asset, liability, owner's equity, revenue, and expense accounts. A typical small business might use the numbers 100–199 for asset accounts, 200–299 for liability accounts, 300–399 for owner's equity accounts, 400–499 for revenue accounts, and 500–599 for expense accounts.

T Accounts

The simplest account structure is shaped like the letter *T*. The account title and account number appear above the T. Debits (abbreviated Dr.) always go on the left side of the T, and credits (abbreviated Cr.) always go on the right.

Account Title	Acct. #
Debit side	Credit side

Accountants record increases in asset, expense, and owner's drawing accounts on the debit side, and they record increases in liability, revenue, and owner's capital accounts on the credit side. An account's assigned **normal balance** is on the side where increases go because the increases in any account are usually greater than the decreases. Therefore, asset, expense, and owner's drawing accounts normally have debit balances. Liability, revenue, and owner's capital accounts normally have credit balances. To determine the correct entry, identify the accounts affected by a transaction, which category each account falls into, and whether the transaction increases or decreases the account's balance. You may find the chart below helpful as a reference.

Assets			Expenses			Owner's Drawing	
Debits	Credits		Debits	Credits		Debits	Credits
Increase	Decrease		Increase	Decrease		Increase	Decrease
Normal Balance			Normal Balance			Normal Balance	

Liabilities			Revenues			Owner's Capital	
Debits	Credits		Debits	Credits		Debits	Credits
Decrease	Increase		Decrease	Increase		Decrease	Increase
	Normal Balance			Normal Balance			Normal Balance

Occasionally, an account does not have a normal balance. For example, a company's checking account (an asset) has a credit balance if the account is overdrawn.

The way people often use the words *debit* and *credit* in everyday speech is not how accountants use these words. For example, the word *credit* generally has positive associations when used conversationally: in school you receive credit for completing a course, a great hockey player may be a credit to his or her team, and a hopeless romantic may at least deserve credit for trying. Someone who is familiar with these uses for *credit* but who is new to accounting may not immediately associate credits with decreases to asset, expense, and owner's drawing accounts. If a business owner loses $5,000 of the company's cash while gambling, the cash account, which is an asset, must be credited for $5,000. (The accountant who records this entry may also deserve credit for realizing that other job offers merit consideration.) For accounting purposes, think of *debit* and *credit* simply in terms of the left-hand and right-hand side of a T account.

Double-Entry Bookkeeping

Under the double-entry bookkeeping system, the full value of each transaction is recorded on the debit side of one or more accounts and also on the credit side of one or more accounts. Therefore, the combined debit balance of all accounts always equals the combined credit balance of all accounts.

Suppose a new company obtains a long-term loan for $50,000 on August 1. The company's cash account (an asset) increases by $50,000, so it is debited for this amount. Simultaneously, the company's notes payable account (a liability) increases by $50,000, so it is credited for this amount. Both sides of the accounting equation increase by $50,000, and total debits and credits remain equal.

Cash	100		Notes Payable	280
Debits	Credits		Debits	Credits
Aug. 1 50,000				Aug. 1 50,000

Some transactions affect only one side of the accounting equation, but the double-entry bookkeeping system nevertheless ensures that the accounting equation remains in balance. For example, if the company pays $30,000 on August 3 to purchase equipment, the cash account's decrease is recorded with a $30,000 credit and the equipment account's increase is recorded with a $30,000 debit. These two asset-account entries offset each other, so the accounting equation remains in balance. Since the cash balance was $50,000 before this transaction occurred, the company has $20,000 in cash after the equipment purchase.

Cash	100
Debits	Credits
Aug. 1 50,000	Aug. 3 30,000
Balance 20,000	

Equipment	110
Debits	Credits
Aug. 3 30,000	

A **compound entry** is necessary when a single transaction affects three or more accounts. Suppose the company's owner purchases a used delivery truck for $20,000 on August 6 by making a $2,000 cash down payment and obtaining a three-year note payable for the remaining $18,000. This transaction is recorded by debiting (increasing) the vehicles account for $20,000, crediting (increasing) the notes payable account for $18,000, and crediting (decreasing) the cash account for $2,000.

Vehicles	120
Debits	Credits
Aug. 6 20,000	

Notes Payable	280
Debits	Credits
	Aug. 1 50,000
	Aug. 6 18,000
	Balance 68,000

Cash	100
Debits	Credits
Aug. 1 50,000	Aug. 3 30,000
	Aug. 6 2,000
Balance 18,000	

The debits and credits total $20,000, and the accounting equation remains in balance because the $18,000 net increase in assets is matched by an $18,000 increase in liabilities. After these three transactions, the company has $68,000 in assets (cash $18,000; equipment $30,000; vehicles $20,000) and $68,000 in liabilities (notes payable).

Journal Entries

Tracking business activity with T accounts would be cumbersome because most businesses have a large number of transactions each day. These transactions are initially recorded on **source documents**, such as invoices or checks. The first step in the accounting process is to analyze each transaction and identify what effect it has on the accounts. After making this determination, an accountant enters the transactions in chronological order into a journal, a process called **journalizing** the transactions. Although many companies use specialized journals for certain transactions, all businesses use a **general journal**. In this book, the terms *general journal* and *journal* are used interchangeably.

The journal's page number appears near the upper right corner. In the example below, GJ1 stands for page 1 of the general journal. Many general journals have five columns: Date, Account Title and Description, Posting Reference, Debit, and Credit.

	General Journal			GJ1
Date	Account Title and Description	Ref.	Debit	Credit
20X1				
Aug. 1	Cash		50,000	
	Notes Payable			50,000
	Borrowed $50,000			
3	Equipment		30,000	
	Cash			30,000
	Purchased equipment			
6	Vehicles		20,000	
	Notes Payable			18,000
	Cash			2,000
	Purchased delivery truck			

To record a **journal entry,** begin by entering the date of the transaction in the journal's date column. For convenience, include the year and month only at the top of each page and next to each month's first entry. In the next column, list each account affected by the transaction on a separate line, and enter a short description of the transaction immediately below the list of accounts. The accounts being debited always appear above the accounts being credited, which are indented slightly. The posting reference column remains blank until the journal entry is transferred to the accounts, a process called **posting**, at which time the account's number is placed in this column. Finally, enter the debit or credit amount for each account in the appropriate columns on the right side of the journal. Generally, one blank line separates each transaction.

The General Ledger

After journalizing transactions, the next step in the accounting process is to post transactions to the accounts in the general ledger. Although T accounts provide a conceptual framework for understanding accounts, most businesses use a more informative and structured spreadsheet layout. A typical account includes date, explanation, and reference columns to the left of the debit column and a balance column to the right of the credit column. The reference column identifies the journal page containing the transaction. The balance column shows the account's balance after every transaction.

			Account Name			Acct. #
Date	Explanation	Ref.	Debit	Credit	Balance

When an account does not have a normal balance, brackets enclose the balance. Assets normally have debit balances, for example, so brackets enclose a checking account's balance only when the account is overdrawn.

As the numbered arrows below indicate, you should post a transaction's first line item to the correct ledger account, completing each column and calculating the account's new balance. Then you should enter the account's reference number in the journal. Repeat this sequence of steps for every account listed in the journal entry.

General Journal   **GJ1**

Date	Account Title and Description	Ref.	Debit	Credit
20X1				
Aug. 1	Cash	100	50,000	
	Notes Payable	280		50,000
	Borrowed $50,000			

(1)   (2)

(4)

Cash   **100**

Date	Explanation	Ref.	Debit	Credit	Balance
20X1					
Aug. 1	Borrowed $50,000	GJ1	50,000		50,000

(3)

Notes Payable   **280**

Date	Explanation	Ref.	Debit	Credit	Balance
20X1					
Aug. 1	Borrowed $50,000	GJ1		50,000	50,000

Referencing the account's number on the journal *after* posting the entry ensures that every line item that has a reference number in the journal has already been posted. This practice can be helpful if phone calls or other distractions interrupt the posting process.

The Recording Process Illustrated

To understand how to record a variety of transactions, consider the description and analysis of the Greener Landscape Group's first thirteen transactions. Then see how each transaction appears in the company's general journal and general ledger accounts.

Transaction 1: On April 1, 20X2, the owner of the Greener Landscape Group, J. Green, invests $15,000 to open the business. Therefore, an asset account (cash) increases and is debited for $15,000, and the owner's capital account (J. Green, capital) increases and is credited for $15,000.

General Journal   GJ1

Date	Account Title and Description	Ref.	Debit	Credit
20X2				
Apr. 1	Cash	100	15,000	
	J. Green, Capital	300		15,000
	Owner investment			

Cash   100

Date	Explanation	Ref.	Debit	Credit	Balance
20X2					
Apr. 1	Owner investment	GJ1	15,000		15,000

J. Green, Capital   300

Date	Explanation	Ref.	Debit	Credit	Balance
20X2					
Apr. 1	Owner investment	GJ1		15,000	15,000

Notice that the cash account has a debit balance and the J. Green, capital account has a credit balance. Since both balances are normal, brackets are not used.

Transaction 2: On April 2, Mr. Green purchases a $15,000 used truck by paying $5,000 in cash and signing a $10,000 note payable, which is due in eighteen months. One asset account (vehicles) increases and is debited for $15,000. Another asset account (cash) decreases and is credited for $5,000. A liability account (notes payable) increases and is credited for $10,000.

The shaded areas below (and in other illustrations in this book) provide a reference for the transaction's position in the journal and ledger accounts. They are not part of the current entry.

General Journal — GJ1

Date	Account Title and Description	Ref.	Debit	Credit
20X2				
Apr. 1	Cash	100	15,000	
	J. Green, Capital	300		15,000
	Owner investment			
2	Vehicles	155	15,000	
	Cash	100		5,000
	Notes Payable	280		10,000
	Purchased truck			

Vehicles — 155

Date	Explanation	Ref.	Debit	Credit	Balance
20X2					
Apr. 2	Acquired truck	GJ1	15,000		15,000

Cash — 100

Date	Explanation	Ref.	Debit	Credit	Balance
20X2					
Apr. 1	Owner investment	GJ1	15,000		15,000
2	Truck downpayment	GJ1		5,000	10,000

Notes Payable — 280

Date	Explanation	Ref.	Debit	Credit	Balance
20X2					
Apr. 2	Loan for truck	GJ1		10,000	10,000

Transaction 3: On April 3, Mr. Green purchases lawn mowers for $3,000 in cash. One asset account (equipment) increases and is debited for $3,000, and another asset account (cash) decreases and is credited for $3,000.

	General Journal			GJ1
Date	Account Title and Description	Ref.	Debit	Credit
2	Vehicles	155	15,000	
	Cash	100		5,000
	Notes Payable	280		10,000
	Purchased truck			
3	Equipment	150	3,000	
	Cash	100		3,000
	Lawnmower purchase			

	Equipment				150
Date	Explanation	Ref.	Debit	Credit	Balance
20X2					
Apr. 3	Lawnmower purchase	GJ1	3,000		3,000

	Cash				100
Date	Explanation	Ref.	Debit	Credit	Balance
20X2					
Apr. 1	Owner investment	GJ1	15,000		15,000
2	Truck downpayment	GJ1		5,000	10,000
3	Lawnmower purchase	GJ1		3,000	7,000

Transaction 4: On April 5, Mr. Green purchases $30 worth of gasoline to power the mowers during April. Since the gas is a cost of doing business during the present accounting period, an expense account (gas expense) increases and is debited for $30. (Remember: increases in asset, expense, and drawing accounts are made with debit entries.) In addition, an asset account (cash) decreases and is credited for $30.

General Journal   GJ1

Date	Account Title and Description	Ref.	Debit	Credit
3	Equipment	150	3,000	
	Cash	100		3,000
	Lawnmower purchase			
5	Gas Expense	510	30	
	Cash	100		30
	Gas for lawnmowers			

Gas Expense   510

Date	Explanation	Ref.	Debit	Credit	Balance
20X2					
Apr. 5	Gas for lawnmowers	GJ1	30		30

Cash   100

Date	Explanation	Ref.	Debit	Credit	Balance
20X2					
Apr. 1	Owner investment	GJ1	15,000		15,000
2	Truck downpayment	GJ1		5,000	10,000
3	Lawnmower purchase	GJ1		3,000	7,000
5	Gas for lawnmowers	GJ1		30	6,970

Transaction 5: On April 5, Mr. Green pays $1,200 for a one-year insurance contract that protects his business from April 1 until March 31 of the following year. Given the length of time this contract is in effect, the matching principle requires that the contract's cost initially be recorded as an asset since it provides a future benefit. Therefore, an asset (prepaid insurance) increases and is debited for $1,200. Another asset account (cash) decreases and is credited for $1,200.

General Journal — GJ1

Date	Account Title and Description	Ref.	Debit	Credit
5	Gas Expense	510	30	
	Cash	100		30
	Gas for lawnmowers			
5	Prepaid Insurance	145	1,200	
	Cash	100		1,200
	Annual insurance premium			

Prepaid Insurance — 145

Date	Explanation	Ref.	Debit	Credit	Balance
20X2					
Apr. 5	Insurance premium	GJ1	1,200		1,200

Cash — 100

Date	Explanation	Ref.	Debit	Credit	Balance
20X2					
Apr. 1	Owner investment	GJ1	15,000		15,000
2	Truck downpayment	GJ1		5,000	10,000
3	Lawnmower purchase	GJ1		3,000	7,000
5	Gas for lawnmowers	GJ1		30	6,970
5	Insurance premium	GJ1		1,200	5,770

Transaction 6: On April 5, Mr. Green purchases $50 worth of office supplies, placing the purchase on his account with the store rather than paying cash. Supplies are a prepaid expense (an asset) until they are used and thereby become a cost of doing business (an expense). Therefore, an asset account (supplies) increases and is debited for $50. Since Mr. Green places the purchase on his account with the store, a liability account (accounts payable) increases and is credited for $50. Accounts payable differ from notes payable. Accounts payable are amounts the company owes based on the good credit of the company or the owner, whereas notes payable are amounts the company owes under formal obligations.

General Journal   GJ1

Date	Account Title and Description	Ref.	Debit	Credit
5	Prepaid Insurance	145	1,200	
	Cash	100		1,200
	Annual insurance premium			
5	Supplies	140	50	
	Accounts Payable	200		50
	Bought office supplies			

Supplies   140

Date	Explanation	Ref.	Debit	Credit	Balance
20X2					
Apr. 5	Bought office supplies	GJ1	50		50

Accounts Payable   200

Date	Explanation	Ref.	Debit	Credit	Balance
20X2					
Apr. 5	Bought office supplies	GJ1		50	50

Transaction 7: On April 14, the Greener Landscape Group cuts grass for seven customers, receiving $50 from each. An asset account (cash) increases and is debited for $350, and a revenue account (lawn cutting revenue) increases and is credited for $350.

General Journal   GJ1

Date	Account Title and Description	Ref.	Debit	Credit
5	Supplies	140	50	
	Accounts Payable	200		50
	Bought office supplies			
14	Cash	100	350	
	Lawn Cutting Revenue	400		350
	Cut seven lawns			

Cash   100

Date	Explanation	Ref.	Debit	Credit	Balance
20X2					
Apr. 1	Owner investment	GJ1	15,000		15,000
2	Truck downpayment	GJ1		5,000	10,000
3	Lawnmower purchase	GJ1		3,000	7,000
5	Gas for lawnmowers	GJ1		30	6,970
5	Insurance premium	GJ1		1,200	5,770
14	Cut seven lawns	GJ1	350		6,120

Lawn Cutting Revenue   400

Date	Explanation	Ref.	Debit	Credit	Balance
20X2					
Apr. 14	Cut seven lawns	GJ1		350	350

Transaction 8: On April 20, Mr. Green receives $270 from a customer for six future maintenance visits. An advance deposit from a customer is an obligation to perform work in the future. It is a liability until the work is performed, at which time it becomes revenue. Therefore, the advance deposit is called unearned revenue. An asset account (cash) increases and is debited for $270, and a liability account (unearned revenue) increases and is credited for $270.

General Journal   GJ1

Date	Account Title and Description	Ref.	Debit	Credit
14	Cash	100	350	
	Lawn Cutting Revenue	400		350
	Cut seven lawns			
20	Cash	100	270	
	Unearned Revenue	250		270
	Prepayment			

Cash   100

Date	Explanation	Ref.	Debit	Credit	Balance
20X2					
Apr. 1	Owner investment	GJ1	15,000		15,000
2	Truck downpayment	GJ1		5,000	10,000
3	Lawnmower purchase	GJ1		3,000	7,000
5	Gas for lawnmowers	GJ1		30	6,970
5	Insurance premium	GJ1		1,200	5,770
14	Cut seven lawns	GJ1	350		6,120
20	Prepayment	GJ1	270		6,390

Unearned Revenue   250

Date	Explanation	Ref.	Debit	Credit	Balance
20X2					
Apr. 20	Prepayment	GJ1		270	270

Transaction 9: On April 22, the Greener Landscape Group cuts grass for eight customers, billing each one $50 but receiving no cash. In accordance with the revenue recognition principle, revenue is recognized upon the completion of a service or the delivery of a product, even if no cash changes hands at that time. Therefore, an asset account (accounts receivable) increases and is debited for $400, and a revenue account (lawn cutting revenue) increases and is credited for $400.

General Journal — GJ2

Date	Account Title and Description	Ref.	Debit	Credit
20X2				
Apr. 22	Accounts Receivable	110	400	
	Lawn Cutting Revenue	400		400
	Cut eight lawns			

Accounts Receivable — 110

Date	Explanation	Ref.	Debit	Credit	Balance
20X2					
Apr. 22	Cut eight lawns	GJ2	400		400

Lawn Cutting Revenue — 400

Date	Explanation	Ref.	Debit	Credit	Balance
20X2					
Apr. 14	Cut seven lawns	GJ1		350	350
22	Cut eight lawns	GJ2		400	750

Notice the new journal page and the corresponding change in posting references on the accounts.

Transaction 10: On April 26, Mr. Green pays $200 in wages to a part-time employee. An expense account (wages expense) increases and is debited for $200, and an asset account (cash) decreases and is credited for $200.

General Journal   GJ2

Date	Account Title and Description	Ref.	Debit	Credit
20X2				
Apr. 22	Accounts Receivable	110	400	
	Lawn Cutting Revenue	400		400
	Cut eight lawns			
26	Wages Expense	500	200	
	Cash	100		200
	Wages through 4-26			

Wages Expense   500

Date	Explanation	Ref.	Debit	Credit	Balance
20X2					
Apr. 26	Wages through 4-26	GJ2	200		200

Cash   100

Date	Explanation	Ref.	Debit	Credit	Balance
20X2					
Apr. 1	Owner investment	GJ1	15,000		15,000
2	Truck downpayment	GJ1		5,000	10,000
3	Lawnmower purchase	GJ1		3,000	7,000
5	Gas for lawnmowers	GJ1		30	6,970
5	Insurance premium	GJ1		1,200	5,770
14	Cut seven lawns	GJ1	350		6,120
20	Prepayment	GJ1	270		6,390
26	Wages through 4-26	GJ2		200	6,190

Transaction 11: On April 28, Mr. Green pays $35 to print advertising fliers. An expense account (advertising expense) increases and is debited for $35, and an asset account (cash) decreases and is credited for $35.

	General Journal				GJ2

Date	Account Title and Description	Ref.	Debit	Credit
26	Wages Expense	500	200	
	Cash	100		200
	Wages through 4-26			
28	Advertising Expense	520	35	
	Cash	100		35
	Printed advertisements			

	Advertising Expense				520

Date	Explanation	Ref.	Debit	Credit	Balance
20X2					
Apr. 28	Printed advertisements	GJ2	35		35

	Cash				100

Date	Explanation	Ref.	Debit	Credit	Balance
20X2					
Apr. 1	Owner investment	GJ1	15,000		15,000
2	Truck downpayment	GJ1		5,000	10,000
3	Lawnmower purchase	GJ1		3,000	7,000
5	Gas for lawnmowers	GJ1		30	6,970
5	Insurance premium	GJ1		1,200	5,770
14	Cut seven lawns	GJ1	350		6,120
20	Prepayment	GJ1	270		6,390
26	Wages through 4-26	GJ2		200	6,190
28	Printed advertisements	GJ2		35	6,155

Transaction 12: On April 29, Mr. Green withdraws $50 for personal use. The owner's drawing account (J. Green, drawing) increases and is debited for $50, and an asset account (cash) decreases and is credited for $50.

General Journal   GJ2

Date	Account Title and Description	Ref.	Debit	Credit
28	Advertising Expense	520	35	
	Cash	100		35
	Printed advertisements			
29	J. Green, Drawing	350	50	
	Cash	100		50
	Owner withdrawal			

J. Green, Drawing   350

Date	Explanation	Ref.	Debit	Credit	Balance
20X2					
Apr. 29	Owner withdrawal	GJ2	50		50

Cash   100

Date	Explanation	Ref.	Debit	Credit	Balance
20X2					
Apr. 1	Owner investment	GJ1	15,000		15,000
2	Truck downpayment	GJ1		5,000	10,000
3	Lawnmower purchase	GJ1		3,000	7,000
5	Gas for lawnmowers	GJ1		30	6,970
5	Annual ins. premium	GJ1		1,200	5,770
14	Cut seven lawns	GJ1	350		6,120
20	Prepayment	GJ1	270		6,390
26	Wages through 4-26	GJ2		200	6,190
28	Printed advertisements	GJ2		35	6,155
29	Owner withdrawal	GJ2		50	6,105

Transaction 13: On April 30, five of the eight previously billed customers each pay $50. Therefore, one asset account (cash) increases and is debited for $250, and another asset account (accounts receivable) decreases and is credited for $250.

General Journal   GJ2

Date	Account Title and Description	Ref.	Debit	Credit
29	J. Green, Drawing	350	50	
	Cash	100		50
	Owner withdrawal			
30	Cash	100	250	
	Accounts Receivable	110		250
	Received customer payments			

Cash   100

Date	Explanation	Ref.	Debit	Credit	Balance
20X2					
Apr. 1	Owner investment	GJ1	15,000		15,000
2	Truck downpayment	GJ1		5,000	10,000
3	Lawnmower purchase	GJ1		3,000	7,000
5	Gas for lawnmowers	GJ1		30	6,970
5	Insurance premium	GJ1		1,200	5,770
14	Cut seven lawns	GJ1	350		6,120
20	Prepayment	GJ1	270		6,390
26	Wages through 4-26	GJ2		200	6,190
28	Printed advertisements	GJ2		35	6,155
29	Owner withdrawal	GJ2		50	6,105
30	Customer payments	GJ2	250		6,355

Accounts Receivable   110

Date	Explanation	Ref.	Debit	Credit	Balance
20X2					
Apr. 22	Cut eight lawns	GJ2	400		400
30	Customer payments	GJ2		250	150

The Trial Balance

After posting all transactions from an accounting period, accountants prepare a **trial balance** to verify that the total of all accounts with debit balances equals the total of all accounts with credit balances. The trial balance lists every open general ledger account by account number and provides separate debit and credit columns for entering account balances. The Greener Landscape Group's trial balance for April 30, 20X2 appears below.

The Greener Landscape Group
Trial Balance
April 30, 20X2

	Account	Debit	Credit
100	Cash	$ 6,355	
110	Accounts Receivable	150	
140	Supplies	50	
145	Prepaid Insurance	1,200	
150	Equipment	3,000	
155	Vehicles	15,000	
200	Accounts Payable		$ 50
250	Unearned Revenue		270
280	Notes Payable		10,000
300	J. Green, Capital		15,000
350	J. Green, Drawing	50	
400	Lawn Cutting Revenue		750
500	Wages Expense	200	
510	Gas Expense	30	
520	Advertising Expense	35	
		$26,070	$26,070

Although dollar signs are not used in journals or ledger accounts, trial balances generally include dollar signs next to the first figure in each column and next to each column's total. Trial balances usually include accounts that had activity during the accounting period but have a zero balance at the end of the period.

An error has occurred when total debits on a trial balance do not equal total credits. There are standard techniques for uncovering some of the errors that cause unequal trial balances. After double-checking each column's total to make sure the problem is not simply an addition error on the trial balance, find the difference between the debit and credit balance totals. If the number *2* divides evenly into this difference, look for an account balance that equals half the difference and that incorrectly appears in the column with the larger total. If the Greener Landscape Group's $50 accounts payable balance were mistakenly put in the debit column, for example, total debits would be $100 greater than total credits on the trial balance.

If the number *9* divides evenly into the difference between the debit and credit balance totals, look for a transposition error in one of the account balances. For example, suppose the cash account's balance of $6,355 were incorrectly entered on the trial balance as $6,535. This would cause total debits to be $180 greater than total credits on the trial balance, an amount evenly divisible by *9* ($180 ÷ 9 = $20). Incidentally, the number of digits in the resulting quotient—the quotient *20* has two digits—always indicates that the transposition error begins this number of digits from the right side of an account balance. Also, the value of the leftmost digit in the quotient—*2* in this case—always equals the difference between the two transposed numbers. Test this by transposing any two adjacent numbers in the trial balance and performing the calculations yourself.

If the difference between the debit and credit balance totals is not divisible by *2* or *9*, look for a ledger account with a balance that equals the difference and is missing from the trial balance. Of course, two or more errors can combine to render these techniques ineffective, and other types of mistakes frequently occur. If the error is not apparent, return to the ledger and recalculate each account's balance. If the error remains, return to the journal and verify that each transaction is posted correctly.

Some errors do not cause the trial balance's column totals to disagree. For example, the columns in a trial balance agree when transactions are not journalized or when journal entries are not posted to the general ledger. Similarly, recording transactions in the wrong accounts does not lead to unequal trial balances. Another common error a trial balance does not catch happens when a single transaction is posted twice. The trial balance is a useful tool, but every transaction must be carefully analyzed, journalized, and posted to ensure the reliability and usefulness of accounting records.

ADJUSTMENTS AND FINANCIAL STATEMENTS

Before financial statements are prepared, additional journal entries, called **adjusting entries,** are made to ensure that the company's financial records adhere to the revenue recognition and matching principles. Adjusting entries are necessary because a single transaction may affect revenues or expenses in more than one accounting period and also because all transactions have not necessarily been documented during the period.

Each adjusting entry usually affects one income statement account (a revenue or expense account) and one balance sheet account (an asset or liability account). For example, suppose a company has a $1,000 debit balance in its supplies account at the end of a month, but a count of supplies on hand finds only $300 of them remaining. Since supplies worth $700 have been used up, the supplies account requires a $700 adjustment so assets are not overstated, and the supplies expense account requires a $700 adjustment so expenses are not understated.

Adjustments fall into one of five categories: accrued revenues, accrued expenses, unearned revenues, prepaid expenses, and depreciation.

Accrued Revenues

An adjusting entry to accrue revenues is necessary when revenues have been earned but not yet recorded. Examples of unrecorded revenues may involve interest revenue and completed services or delivered goods that, for any number of reasons, have not been billed to customers. Suppose a customer owes 6% interest on a three-year, $10,000 note receivable but has not yet made any payments. At the end of each accounting period, the company recognizes the interest revenue that has accrued on this long-term receivable.

Unless otherwise specified, interest is calculated with the following formula: principal × annual interest rate × time period in years.

$$\$10{,}000 \times 6\% \times \frac{30}{360} = \$50$$

Most textbooks use a 360-day year for interest calculations, which is done here. In practice, however, most lenders make more precise calculations by using a 365-day year.

Since the company accrues $50 in interest revenue during the month, an adjusting entry is made to increase (debit) an asset account (interest receivable) by $50 and to increase (credit) a revenue account (interest revenue) by $50.

General Journal   GJ3

Date	Account Title and Description	Ref.	Debit	Credit
20X7				
Apr. 30	Interest Receivable	115	50	
	Interest Revenue	420		50
	Accrue interest			

Interest Receivable   115

Date	Explanation	Ref.	Debit	Credit	Balance
20X7					
Apr. 30	Accrue interest	GJ3	50		50

Interest Revenue   420

Date	Explanation	Ref.	Debit	Credit	Balance
20X7					
Apr. 30	Accrue interest	GJ3		50	50

If a plumber does $90 worth of work for a customer on the last day of April but doesn't send a bill until May 4, the revenue should be recognized in April's accounting records. Therefore, the plumber makes an adjusting entry to increase (debit) accounts receivable for $90 and to increase (credit) service revenue for $90.

General Journal   GJ4

Date	Account Title and Description	Ref.	Debit	Credit
20X7				
Apr. 30	Accounts Receivable	110	90	
	Service Revenue	400		90
	Accrue unbilled service			

Accounts Receivable   110

Date	Explanation	Ref.	Debit	Credit	Balance
20X7					3,610
Apr. 30	Accrue unbilled service	GJ4	90		3,700

Service Revenue   400

Date	Explanation	Ref.	Debit	Credit	Balance
20X7					12,100
Apr. 30	Accrue unbilled service	GJ4		90	12,190

Accounting records that do not include adjusting entries for accrued revenues understate total assets, total revenues, and net income.

Accrued Expenses

An adjusting entry to accrue expenses is necessary when there are unrecorded expenses and liabilities that apply to a given accounting period. These expenses may include wages for work performed in the current accounting period but not paid until the following accounting period and also the accumulation of interest on notes payable and other debts.

Suppose a company owes its employees $2,000 in unpaid wages at the end of an accounting period. The company makes an adjusting entry to accrue the expense by increasing (debiting) wages expense for $2,000 and by increasing (crediting) wages payable for $2,000.

General Journal — GJ9

Date	Account Title and Description	Ref.	Debit	Credit
20X7				
Oct. 31	Wages Expense	500	2,000	
	Wages Payable	270		2,000
	Accrue wages			

Wages Expense — 500

Date	Explanation	Ref.	Debit	Credit	Balance
20X7					20,000
Oct. 31	Accrue wages	GJ9	2,000		22,000

Wages Payable — 270

Date	Explanation	Ref.	Debit	Credit	Balance
20X7					
Oct. 31	Accrue wages	GJ9		2,000	2,000

If a long-term note payable of $10,000 carries an annual interest rate of 12%, then $1,200 in interest expense accrues each year. At the close of each month, therefore, the company makes an adjusting entry to increase (debit) interest expense for $100 and to increase (credit) interest payable for $100.

General Journal   GJ5

Date	Account Title and Description	Ref.	Debit	Credit
20X7				
May 31	Interest Expense	530	100	
	Interest Payable	220		100
	Accrue interest			

Interest Expense   530

Date	Explanation	Ref.	Debit	Credit	Balance
20X7					
May 31	Accrue interest	GJ5	100		100

Interest Payable   220

Date	Explanation	Ref.	Debit	Credit	Balance
20X7					
May 31	Accrue interest	GJ5		100	100

Accounting records that do not include adjusting entries for accrued expenses understate total liabilities and total expenses and overstate net income.

Unearned Revenues

Unearned revenues are payments for future services to be performed or goods to be delivered. Advance customer payments for newspaper subscriptions or extended warranties are unearned revenues at the time of sale. At the end of each accounting period, adjusting entries must be made to recognize the portion of unearned revenues that have been earned during the period.

Suppose a customer pays $1,800 for an insurance policy to protect her delivery vehicles for six months. Initially, the insurance company records this transaction by increasing an asset account (cash) with a debit and by increasing a liability account (unearned revenue) with a credit. After one month, the insurance company makes an adjusting entry to decrease (debit) unearned revenue and to increase (credit) revenue by an amount equal to one sixth of the initial payment.

	General Journal				GJ1
Date	Account Title and Description	Ref.	Debit	Credit	
20X7					
Jan. 31	Unearned Insurance Revenue	250	300		
	Vehicle Insurance Revenue	425		300	
	Earned insurance premiums				

	Unearned Insurance Revenue				250
Date	Explanation	Ref.	Debit	Credit	Balance
20X7					1,800
Jan. 31	Earned premiums	GJ1	300		1,500

	Vehicle Insurance Revenue				425
Date	Explanation	Ref.	Debit	Credit	Balance
20X7					
Jan. 31	Earned premiums	GJ1		300	300

Accounting records that do not include adjusting entries to show the earning of previously unearned revenues overstate total liabilities and understate total revenues and net income.

Prepaid Expenses

Prepaid expenses are assets that become expenses as they expire or get used up. For example, office supplies are considered an asset until they are used in the course of doing business, at which time they become an expense. At the end of each accounting period, adjusting entries are necessary to recognize the portion of prepaid expenses that have become actual expenses through use or the passage of time.

Consider the previous example from the point of view of the customer who pays $1,800 for six months of insurance coverage. Initially, she records the transaction by increasing one asset account (prepaid insurance) with a debit and by decreasing another asset account (cash) with a credit. After one month, she makes an adjusting entry to increase (debit) insurance expense for $300 and to decrease (credit) prepaid insurance for $300.

General Journal   GJ1

Date	Account Title and Description	Ref.	Debit	Credit
20X7				
Jan. 31	Insurance Expense	550	300	
	Prepaid Insurance	145		300
	Expired insurance			

Insurance Expense   550

Date	Explanation	Ref.	Debit	Credit	Balance
20X7					
Jan. 31	Expired insurance	GJ1	300		300

Prepaid Insurance   145

Date	Explanation	Ref.	Debit	Credit	Balance
20X7					1,800
Jan. 31	Expired insurance	GJ1		300	1,500

Prepaid expenses in one company's accounting records are often—but not always—unearned revenues in another company's accounting records. Office supplies provide an example of a prepaid expense that does not appear on another company's books as unearned revenue.

Accounting records that do not include adjusting entries to show the expiration or consumption of prepaid expenses overstate assets and net income and understate expenses.

Depreciation

Depreciation is the process of allocating the depreciable cost of a long-lived asset, except for land which is never depreciated, to expense over the asset's estimated service life. **Depreciable cost** includes all costs necessary to acquire an asset and make it ready for use minus the asset's expected **salvage value,** which is the asset's worth at the end of its **service life,** usually the amount of time the asset is expected to be used in the business. For example, if a truck costs $30,000, has an expected salvage value of $6,000, and has an estimated service life of sixty months, then $24,000 is allocated to expense at a rate of $400 each month ($24,000 ÷ 60 = $400). This method of calculating depreciation expense, called **straight-line depreciation,** is the simplest and most widely used method for financial reporting purposes. However, several other methods of calculating depreciation expense are discussed on pages 178–190.

Some accountants treat depreciation as a special type of prepaid expense because the adjusting entries have the same effect on the accounts. Accounting records that do not include adjusting entries for depreciation expense overstate assets and net income and understate expenses. Nevertheless, most accountants consider depreciation to be a distinct type of adjustment because of the special account structure used to report depreciation expense on the balance sheet.

Since the original cost of a long-lived asset should always be readily identifiable, a different type of balance-sheet account, called a **contra-asset account,** is used to record depreciation expense. Increases and normal balances appear on the credit side of a contra-asset account. The **net book value** of long-lived assets is found by subtracting the contra-asset account's credit balance from the corresponding asset account's debit balance. Do not confuse book value with market value. Book value is the portion of the asset's cost that has not been written off to expense. **Market value** is the price someone would pay for the asset. These two values are usually different.

Suppose an accountant calculates that a $125,000 piece of equipment depreciates by $1,000 each month. After one month, he makes an adjusting entry to increase (debit) an expense account (depreciation expense–equipment) by $1,000 and to increase (credit) a contra-asset account (accumulated depreciation–equipment) by $1,000.

General Journal — GJ10

Date	Account Title and Description	Ref.	Debit	Credit
20X7				
Dec. 31	Depreciation Expense–Equipment	560	1,000	
	Accumulated Depreciation–Equipment	160		1,000
	Monthly depreciation			

Depreciation Expense–Equipment — 560

Date	Explanation	Ref.	Debit	Credit	Balance
20X7					
Dec. 31	Monthly depreciation	GJ10	1,000		1,000

Accumulated Depreciation–Equipment — 160

Date	Explanation	Ref.	Debit	Credit	Balance
20X7					
Dec. 31	Monthly depreciation	GJ10		1,000	1,000

On a balance sheet, the accumulated depreciation account's balance is subtracted from the equipment account's balance to show the equipment's net book value.

ACME Manufacturing
Partial Balance Sheet
December 31, 20X7

Property, Plant, and Equipment
Equipment	125,000	
Less: Accumulated Depreciation	(1,000)	124,000

The Adjustment Process Illustrated

Accountants prepare a trial balance both before and after making adjusting entries. Reexamine the Greener Landscape Group's unadjusted trial balance for April 30, 20X2.

The Greener Landscape Group
Trial Balance
April 30, 20X2

	Account	Debit	Credit
100	Cash	$ 6,355	
110	Accounts Receivable	150	
140	Supplies	50	
145	Prepaid Insurance	1,200	
150	Equipment	3,000	
155	Vehicles	15,000	
200	Accounts Payable		$ 50
250	Unearned Revenue		270
280	Notes Payable		10,000
300	J. Green, Capital		15,000
350	J. Green, Drawing	50	
400	Lawn Cutting Revenue		750
500	Wages Expense	200	
510	Gas Expense	30	
520	Advertising Expense	35	
		$26,070	$26,070

Consider eight adjusting entries recorded in Mr. Green's general journal and posted to his general ledger accounts. Then, see the **adjusted trial balance,** which shows the balance of all accounts after the adjusting entries are journalized and posted to the general ledger accounts.

Adjustment A: During the afternoon of April 30, Mr. Green cuts one lawn, and he agrees to mail the customer a bill for $50, which he does on May 2. In accordance with the revenue recognition principle (page 12), Mr. Green makes an adjusting entry in April to increase (debit) accounts receivable for $50 and to increase (credit) lawn cutting revenue for $50.

General Journal — GJ2

Date	Account Title and Description	Ref.	Debit	Credit
30	Cash	100	250	
	Accounts Receivable	110		250
	Received customer payments			
30	Accounts Receivable	110	50	
	Lawn Cutting Revenue	400		50
	Accrue unbilled revenue			

Accounts Receivable — 110

Date	Explanation	Ref.	Debit	Credit	Balance
20X2					
Apr. 22	Cut eight lawns	GJ2	400		400
30	Customer payments	GJ2		250	150
30	Accrue unbilled revenue	GJ2	50		200

Lawn Cutting Revenue — 400

Date	Explanation	Ref.	Debit	Credit	Balance
20X2					
Apr. 14	Cut seven lawns	GJ1		350	350
22	Cut eight lawns	GJ2		400	750
30	Accrue unbilled revenue	GJ2		50	800

Adjustment B: Mr. Green's $10,000 note payable, which he signed on April 2, carries a 10.2% interest rate. Interest calculations usually exclude the day that loans occur and include the day that loans are paid off. Therefore, Mr. Green uses the formula below to calculate how much interest expense accrued during the final twenty-eight days of April.

$$\$10,000 \times 10.2\% \times \frac{28}{360} = \$79$$

Since the matching principle requires that expenses be reported in the accounting period to which they apply, Mr. Green makes an adjusting entry to increase (debit) interest expense for $79 and to increase (credit) interest payable for $79.

General Journal — GJ2

Date	Account Title and Description	Ref.	Debit	Credit
30	Accounts Receivable	110	50	
	Lawn Cutting Revenue	400		50
	Accrue unbilled revenue			
30	Interest Expense	530	79	
	Interest Payable	220		79
	Accrue interest			

Interest Expense — 530

Date	Explanation	Ref.	Debit	Credit	Balance
20X2					
Apr. 30	Accrue interest	GJ2	79		79

Interest Payable — 220

Date	Explanation	Ref.	Debit	Credit	Balance
20X2					
Apr. 30	Accrue interest	GJ2		79	79

Adjustment C: Mr. Green's part-time employee earns $80 during the last four days of April but will not be paid until May 10. This requires an adjusting entry that increases (debits) wages expense for $80 and that increases (credits) wages payable for $80.

General Journal — GJ2

Date	Account Title and Description	Ref.	Debit	Credit
30	Interest Expense	530	79	
	Interest Payable	220		79
	Accrue interest			
30	Wages Expense	500	80	
	Wages Payable	210		80
	Accrue wages 4-27 to 4-30			

Wages Expense — 500

Date	Explanation	Ref.	Debit	Credit	Balance
20X2					
Apr. 26	Wages through 4-26	GJ2	200		200
30	Accrue wages 4-27 to 4-30	GJ2	80		280

Wages Payable — 210

Date	Explanation	Ref.	Debit	Credit	Balance
20X2					
Apr. 30	Accrue wages 4-27 to 4-30	GJ2		80	80

Adjustment D: On April 20 Mr. Green received a $270 prepayment for six future visits. Assuming Mr. Green completed one of these visits in April, he must make a $45 adjusting entry to decrease (debit) unearned revenue and to increase (credit) lawn cutting revenue.

General Journal   GJ3

Date	Account Title and Description	Ref.	Debit	Credit
20X2				
Apr. 30	Unearned Revenue	250	45	
	Lawn Cutting Revenue	400		45
	Earned revenue			

Unearned Revenue   250

Date	Explanation	Ref.	Debit	Credit	Balance
20X2					
Apr. 20	Prepayment	GJ1		270	270
30	Earned revenue	GJ3	45		225

Lawn Cutting Revenue   400

Date	Explanation	Ref.	Debit	Credit	Balance
20X2					
Apr. 14	Cut seven lawns	GJ1		350	350
22	Cut eight lawns	GJ2		400	750
30	Accrue unbilled revenue	GJ2		50	800
30	Earned revenue	GJ3		45	845

Adjustment E: Mr. Green discovers that he used $25 worth of office supplies during April. He therefore makes a $25 adjusting entry to increase (debit) supplies expense and to decrease (credit) supplies.

General Journal   GJ3

Date	Account Title and Description	Ref.	Debit	Credit
20X2				
Apr. 30	Unearned Revenue	250	45	
	Lawn Cutting Revenue	400		45
	Earned revenue			
30	Supplies Expense	540	25	
	Supplies	140		25
	Supplies used			

Supplies Expense   540

Date	Explanation	Ref.	Debit	Credit	Balance
20X2					
Apr. 30	Supplies used	GJ3	25		25

Supplies   140

Date	Explanation	Ref.	Debit	Credit	Balance
20X2					
Apr. 5	Bought office supplies	GJ1	50		50
30	Supplies used	GJ3		25	25

Adjustment F: Mr. Green must record the expiration of one twelfth of his company's insurance policy. Since the annual premium is $1,200, he makes a $100 adjusting entry to increase (debit) insurance expense and to decrease (credit) prepaid insurance.

General Journal   GJ3

Date	Account Title and Description	Ref.	Debit	Credit
30	Supplies Expense	540	25	
	Supplies	140		25
	Supplies used			
30	Insurance Expense	545	100	
	Prepaid Insurance	145		100
	Expired insurance			

Insurance Expense   545

Date	Explanation	Ref.	Debit	Credit	Balance
20X2					
Apr. 30	Expired insurance	GJ3	100		100

Prepaid Insurance   145

Date	Explanation	Ref.	Debit	Credit	Balance
20X2					
Apr. 5	Insurance premium	GJ1	1,200		1,200
30	Expired insurance	GJ3		100	1,100

Adjustment G: If depreciation expense on Mr. Green's $15,000 truck is $200 each month, he makes a $200 adjusting entry to increase (debit) an expense account (depreciation expense–vehicles) and to increase (credit) a contra-asset account (accumulated depreciation–vehicles).

General Journal GJ3

Date	Account Title and Description	Ref.	Debit	Credit
30	Insurance Expense	550	100	
	Prepaid Insurance	145		100
	Expired insurance			
30	Depreciation Expense–Vehicles	556	200	
	Accumulated Depreciation–Vehicles	156		200
	Monthly vehicle depreciation			

Depreciation Expense–Vehicles 556

Date	Explanation	Ref.	Debit	Credit	Balance
20X2					
Apr. 30	Monthly depreciation	GJ3	200		200

Accumulated Depreciation–Vehicles 156

Date	Explanation	Ref.	Debit	Credit	Balance
20X2					
Apr. 30	Monthly depreciation	GJ3		200	200

The truck's net book value is now $14,800, which is calculated by subtracting the $200 credit balance in the accumulated depreciation–vehicles account from the $15,000 debit balance in the vehicles account. Many accountants calculate the depreciation of long-lived assets to the nearest month. Had Mr. Green purchased the truck on April 16 or later, he might not make this adjusting entry until the end of May.

Adjustment H: If depreciation expense on Mr. Green's equipment is $35 each month, he makes a $35 adjusting entry to increase (debit) depreciation expense–equipment and to increase (credit) accumulated depreciation–equipment.

General Journal · GJ3

Date	Account Title and Description	Ref.	Debit	Credit
30	Depreciation Expense–Vehicles	556	200	
	Accumulated Depreciation–Vehicles	156		200
	Monthly vehicle depreciation			
30	Depreciation Expense–Equipment	551	35	
	Accumulated Depreciation–Equipment	151		35
	Monthly equipment depreciation			

Depreciation Expense–Equipment · 551

Date	Explanation	Ref.	Debit	Credit	Balance
20X2					
Apr. 30	Monthly depreciation	GJ3	35		35

Accumulated Depreciation–Equipment · 151

Date	Explanation	Ref.	Debit	Credit	Balance
20X2					
Apr. 30	Monthly depreciation	GJ3		35	35

After journalizing and posting all of the adjusting entries, Mr. Green prepares an adjusted trial balance. The Greener Landscape Group's adjusted trial balance for April 30, 20X2 appears below.

The Greener Landscape Group
Adjusted Trial Balance
April 30, 20X2

Account		Debit	Credit
100	Cash	$ 6,355	
110	Accounts Receivable	200	
140	Supplies	25	
145	Prepaid Insurance	1,100	
150	Equipment	3,000	
151	Accumulated Depreciation–Equipment		$ 35
155	Vehicles	15,000	
156	Accumulated Depreciation–Vehicles		200
200	Accounts Payable		50
210	Wages Payable		80
220	Interest Payable		79
250	Unearned Revenue		225
280	Notes Payable		10,000
300	J. Green, Capital		15,000
350	J. Green, Drawing	50	
400	Lawn Cutting Revenue		845
500	Wages Expense	280	
510	Gas Expense	30	
520	Advertising Expense	35	
530	Interest Expense	79	
540	Supplies Expense	25	
545	Insurance Expense	100	
551	Depreciation Expense–Equipment	35	
556	Depreciation Expense–Vehicles	200	
		$26,514	$26,514

Financial Statements

Financial statements are prepared immediately after the adjusted trial balance. Although the first chapter of this book introduces the four basic financial statements, knowing how to record transactions, make adjusting entries, and create trial balances gives you a greater understanding of the information financial statements contain.

Income statement. The income statement, which is sometimes called the statement of earnings or statement of operations, lists all revenue and expense account balances and shows the company's net income or net loss for a particular period of time. This statement may be prepared using a single-step or multiple-step format. The single-step format puts revenue and expense accounts into separate groups. Then, total expenses are subtracted from total revenues to determine the net income or loss.

The Greener Landscape Group
Income Statement
For the Month Ended April 30, 20X2

Revenues		
Lawn Cutting Revenue		$845
Expenses		
Wages Expense	$280	
Depreciation Expense–Vehicles	200	
Insurance Expense	100	
Interest Expense	79	
Depreciation Expense–Equipment	35	
Advertising Expense	35	
Gas Expense	30	
Supplies Expense	25	
Total Expenses		784
Net Income		$ 61

The multiple-step format uses the same accounts and balances but separates the cost of services provided from operating expenses and also includes a category for other types of income and expense.

The Greener Landscape Group
Income Statement
For the Month Ended April 30, 20X2

Revenues		
Lawn Cutting Revenue		$845
Cost of Services Provided		
Wages Expense	$280	
Depreciation Expense–Vehicles	200	
Insurance Expense	100	
Depreciation Expense–Equipment	35	
Gas Expense	30	
Total Cost of Services Provided		645
Gross Profit		200
Operating Expenses		
Advertising Expense	35	
Supplies Expense	25	
Total Operating Expenses		60
Operating Income		140
Other Income/(Expense), Net		
Interest Expense		(79)
Net Income		$ 61

Companies may use slightly different categories for expenses, but the overall structure for this type of income statement is essentially the same. For example, merchandising companies include a category for the cost of goods sold, and many companies break operating expenses into two subcategories: selling expenses and general and administrative expenses.

Statement of owner's equity. The statement of owner's equity shows activity in the owner's equity accounts for a particular period of time. The capital account's opening balance is followed by a list of increases and decreases, and the account's closing balance is calculated from this information. Increases include investments made by the owner and net income. Decreases include owner withdrawals and net loss. Since the income statement already shows all revenue and expense account balances, only the company's net income or loss appears on this statement.

The Greener Landscape Group
Statement of Owner's Equity
For the Month Ended April 30, 20X2

J. Green, Capital, April 1		$ 0
Additions		
Investments	$15,000	
Net Income	61	15,061
Withdrawals		(50)
J. Green, Capital, April 30		$15,011

Balance sheet. The balance sheet lists the asset, liability, and owner's equity balances at a specific time. It proves that the accounting equation (Assets = Liabilities + Owner's Equity) is in balance. The ending balance on the statement of owner's equity is used to report owner's equity on the balance sheet.

The Greener Landscape Group
Balance Sheet
April 30, 20X2

Assets		
Cash		$ 6,355
Accounts Receivable		200
Supplies		25
Prepaid Insurance		1,100
Vehicles	$15,000	
Less: Accumulated Depreciation	(200)	
Equipment	3,000	
Less: Accumulated Depreciation	(35)	17,765
Total Assets		$25,445
Liabilities and Owner's Equity		
Liabilities		
Accounts Payable		$ 50
Wages Payable		80
Interest Payable		79
Unearned Revenue		225
Notes Payable		10,000
Total Liabilities		10,434
Owner's Equity		
J. Green, Capital		15,011
Total Liabilities and Owner's Equity		$25,445

To aid readers, most companies prepare a classified balance sheet, which categorizes assets and liabilities. The standard asset categories on a classified balance sheet are current assets; property, plant, and equipment; long-term investments; and intangible assets. Liabilities are generally divided into current liabilities and long-term liabilities. The first chapter includes a detailed description of these categories.

The Greener Landscape Group
Balance Sheet
April 30, 20X2

ASSETS

Current Assets

Cash			$ 6,355
Accounts Receivable			200
Supplies			25
Prepaid Insurance			1,100
Total Current Assets			7,680

Property, Plant, and Equipment

Vehicles	$15,000		
Less: Accumulated Depreciation	(200)	$14,800	
Vehicles	3,000		
Less: Accumulated Depreciation	(35)	2,965	17,765
Total Assets			$25,445

LIABILITIES AND OWNER'S EQUITY

Current Liabilities

Accounts Payable		$ 50
Wages Payable		80
Interest Payable		79
Unearned Revenue		225
Total Current Liabilities		434

Long-Term Liabilities

Notes Payable		10,000
Total Liabilities		10,434

Owner's Equity

J. Green, Capital		15,011
Total Liabilities and Owner's Equity		$25,445

Statement of cash flows. The statement of cash flows places all cash exchanges into one of three categories—operating, investing, or financing—to calculate the net change in cash during the accounting period. **Operating cash flows** arise from day-to-day business operations such as inventory purchases, sales revenue, and payroll expenses. Note that interest and dividends received from long-term assets (investing activities) and interest payments for long-term loans (financing activities) appear on the income statement, so they would appear as operating cash flows on the statement of cash flows. Income taxes are also included with operating cash flows. **Investing cash flows** relate to cash exchanges involving long-term assets, such as the purchase or sale of land, buildings, equipment, or long-term investments in another company's stock or debt. **Financing cash flows** involve changes in long-term liabilities and owner's equity. Examples include the receipt or early retirement of long-term loans, the sale or repurchase of stock, and the payment of dividends to shareholders.

The Greener Landscape Group
Statement of Cash Flows
For the Month Ended April 30, 20X2

Cash Flows from Operating Activities	
Cash from Customers	$ 870
Cash to Employees	(200)
Cash to Suppliers	(1,265)
Cash Flow Used by Operating Activities	(595)
Cash Flows from Investing Activities	
Purchase of Vehicle	(5,000)
Purchase of Equipment	(3,000)
Cash Flow Used by Investing Activities	(8,000)
Cash Flows from Financing Activities	
Investment by Owner	15,000
Withdrawal by Owner	(50)
Cash Flow Provided by Financing Activities	14,950
Net Increase in Cash	6,355
Beginning Cash, April 1	0
Ending Cash, April 30	$ 6,355

Noncash Financing and Investing Activity
  The company purchased a used truck for $15,000, paying $5,000 in cash and signing a note for the remaining balance. The note payable portion of the transaction is not included on this statement.

As its name implies, this statement focuses on cash flows rather than income. For example, the $870 Mr. Green receives from customers includes unearned revenues and excludes accounts receivable. At the bottom of the statement, the net increase or decrease in cash is used to reconcile the accounting period's beginning and ending cash balances. Significant noncash transactions likely to impact cash flow in other accounting periods must also be disclosed, but this does not occur in the body of the statement. The footnote in the illustration shows one way to accomplish such disclosures.

According to current accounting standards, operating cash flows may be disclosed using either the direct or the indirect method. The **direct method,** which appears in the illustration on the previous page, simply lists operating cash flows by type of cash receipt and payment. The direct method is straightforward and easy to interpret, but only a small percentage of companies actually use this method. *Cliffs Quick Review Accounting Principles II* explains the indirect method in detail, but a short description of the indirect method is worth mentioning here because most companies use it. The **indirect method** reports operating cash flows by listing the company's net income or loss and then adjusting this figure because net income is not calculated on the cash basis.

COMPLETION OF THE ACCOUNTING CYCLE

The Work Sheet

Many accountants use a work sheet to prepare the unadjusted trial balance, to assign the adjusting entries to the correct accounts, to create the adjusted trial balance, and then to prepare preliminary financial statements. A work sheet is an optional step in the accounting cycle. It is an informal document that is not considered a financial statement, although it gives management some information about results for a period. Work sheets usually have five sets of debit and credit columns, which are completed from left to right one set at a time. Turn the page to see the Greener Landscape Group's work sheet for the month of April.

Use the first set of columns to prepare a trial balance. List all open accounts on the left side of the work sheet and enter each account's debit or credit balance in the appropriate columns immediately to the right. The trial balance in the sample work sheet includes the same information as the trial balance shown on page 38.

The second set of columns shows how the adjusting entries affect the accounts. While completing these columns, list additional accounts as needed along the left side of the work sheet. Use a letter to index the debit and credit portion of each adjusting entry so that, later, it is easier to journalize and post the adjustments. An explanation of each adjustment may be written at the bottom of the work sheet. If an account has more than one adjustment, each is shown separately, using as many lines as necessary. After entering all the adjustments on the work sheet, make sure the column totals are equal.

The third set of columns contains the adjusted trial balance. The adjusted account balances in these columns equal the sum of the trial balance and adjustments columns. Consider the first three accounts on the Greener Landscape Group's work sheet. Since no adjustments affect the cash account, that account's debit balance carries across to the debit column of the adjusted trial balance. Accounts receivable begins with a $150 debit balance and has a $50 debit in the adjustments column. These amounts combine to give the account a $200 debit balance in the adjusted trial balance. In the supplies account, a $50 debit balance combines with a $25 credit in the adjustments column to yield a $25 debit balance. Although each individual account works this way, the totals at the bottom of the trial balance and adjustments columns cannot be combined to determine the column totals at the bottom of the adjusted trial balance—adding $26,070 to $614 clearly does not yield $26,514. After entering each balance in the work sheet's adjusted trial balance, total each column to make sure the debits and credits are equal.

Each account's adjusted trial balance transfers directly to either the fourth or fifth set of columns. Move all revenue and expense account balances to the income statement columns, and move all other account balances (assets, liabilities, owner's capital, and owner's drawing) to the balance sheet columns. Then total each of the final four columns. Unless net income is zero, the columns have unequal debit and credit totals. If total credits are greater than total debits in the income statement columns, the company has net income, and the difference between these columns is added to the work sheet's income statement debit column and balance sheet credit column on a line labeled *Net Income*. The difference is added to the balance sheet credit column because net income increases owner's equity, and increases to owner's equity are recorded with credits. If total debits are greater than total credits in the income statement columns, a net loss occurs, and the difference between these column totals is added to the work sheet's income statement credit column and balance sheet debit column on a line labeled *Net Loss*. Once the company's net income or net loss is added to the correct income statement and balance sheet columns, each set of debit and credit columns balance, and the work sheet is complete.

Prepare the income statement, statement of owner's equity, and balance sheet from the completed work sheet. The accounts and balances in the work sheet's income statement columns transfer directly to the income statement, which is prepared first. Next, from the work sheet's balance sheet columns, use the owner's capital and drawing account balances and the company's net income or loss to complete the statement of owner's equity. Complete the balance sheet last. When

The Greener Landscape Group
Work Sheet
For the Month Ended April 30, 20X2

Account	Trial Balance Dr.	Trial Balance Cr.	Adjustments Dr.	Adjustments Cr.	Adjusted Trial Balance Dr.	Adjusted Trial Balance Cr.	Income Statement Dr.	Income Statement Cr.	Balance Sheet Dr.	Balance Sheet Cr.
	6,355				6,355				6,355	
	150		50 (a)		200				200	
	50			25 (e)	25				25	
	1,200			100 (f)	1,100				1,100	
	3,000				3,000				3,000	
	15,000				15,000				15,000	
		50				50				2
		270	45 (d)			225				
		10,000				10,000				10,0
		15,000				15,000				15,0
	50				50				50	
		750		50 (a)		845		845		
				45 (d)						
	200		80 (c)		280		280			
	30				30		30			
	35				35		35			
	26,070	26,070								
			79 (b)		79		79			
				79 (b)		79				
				80 (c)		80				
			25 (e)		25		25			
			100 (f)		100		100			
hicles			200 (g)		200		200			
-Vehicles				200 (g)		200				2
uipment			35 (h)		35		35			
-Equipment				35 (h)		35				
			614	614	26,514	26,514	784	845	25,730	25,6
							61			
							845	845	25,730	25,7

preparing the balance sheet, be careful *not* to use the capital account balance on the work sheet because it shows the capital account's beginning balance for the accounting period. Instead, use the ending balance on the statement of owner's equity, which has already adjusted the capital account's balance to reflect the company's net income or loss and any withdrawals made by the owner. After the financial statements are prepared, the adjusting entries are journalized and posted.

Closing Entries

To update the balance in the owner's capital account, accountants close revenue, expense, and drawing accounts at the end of each fiscal year or, occasionally, at the end of each accounting period. For this reason, these types of accounts are called **temporary** or **nominal accounts.** Assets, liabilities, and the owner's capital account, in contrast, are called **permanent** or **real accounts** because their ending balance in one accounting period is always the starting balance in the subsequent accounting period. When an accountant closes an account, the account balance returns to zero. Starting with zero balances in the temporary accounts each year makes it easier to track revenues, expenses, and withdrawals and to compare them from one year to the next. There are four **closing entries,** which transfer all temporary account balances to the owner's capital account.

1. Close the income statement accounts with credit balances (normally revenue accounts) to a special temporary account named *income summary.*

2. Close the income statement accounts with debit balances (normally expense accounts) to the income summary account. After all revenue and expense accounts are closed, the income summary account's balance equals the company's net income or loss for the period.

3. Close income summary to the owner's capital account or, in corporations, to the retained earnings account. The purpose of the income summary account is simply to keep the permanent owner's capital or retained earnings account uncluttered.

4. Close the owner's drawing account to the owner's capital account. In corporations, this entry closes any dividend accounts to the retained earnings account. For purposes of illustration, closing entries for the Greener Landscape Group appear on the next several pages.

Closing entry 1: The lawn cutting revenue account is Mr. Green's only income statement account with a credit balance. Debit this account for an amount equal to the account's balance, and credit income summary for the same amount.

General Journal GJ3

Date	Account Title and Description	Ref.	Debit	Credit
30	Depreciation Expense–Equipment	551	35	
	Accumulated Depreciation–Equipment	151		35
	Monthly equipment depreciation			
	Closing Entries			
Apr. 30	Lawn Cutting Revenue	400	845	
	Income Summary	600		845
	Close credit-balance accounts			

Lawn Cutting Revenue 400

Date	Explanation	Ref.	Debit	Credit	Balance
20X2					
Apr. 14	Cut seven lawns	GJ1		350	350
22	Cut eight lawns	GJ2		400	750
30	Accrue unbilled revenue	GJ2		50	800
30	Earned revenue	GJ3		45	845
30	Closing entry	GJ3	845		0

Income Summary 600

Date	Explanation	Ref.	Debit	Credit	Balance
20X2					
Apr. 30	Credit-balance accounts	GJ3		845	845

Closing entry 2: Mr. Green has eight income statement accounts with debit balances; they are all expense accounts. Close these accounts by debiting income summary for an amount equal to the combined

General Journal GJ4

Date	Account Title and Description	Ref.	Debit	Credit
20X2				
Apr. 30	Income Summary	600	784	
	Wages Expense	500		280
	Gas Expense	510		30
	Advertising Expense	520		35
	Interest Expense	530		79
	Supplies Expense	540		25
	Insurance Expense	545		100
	Depreciation Expense–Equipment	551		35
	Depreciation Expense–Vehicles	556		200
	Close debit-balance accounts			

Income Summary 600

Date	Explanation	Ref.	Debit	Credit	Balance
20X2					
Apr. 30	Credit-balance accounts	GJ3		845	845
30	Debit-balance accounts	GJ4	784		61

Wages Expense 500

Date	Explanation	Ref.	Debit	Credit	Balance
20X2					
Apr. 26	Wages through 4-26	GJ2	200		200
30	Accrue wages 4-27 to 4-30	GJ2	80		280
30	Closing entry	GJ4		280	0

Gas Expense 510

Date	Explanation	Ref.	Debit	Credit	Balance
20X2					
Apr. 5	Gas for lawnmowers	GJ1	30		30
30	Closing entry	GJ4		30	0

debit balances of all eight expense accounts and by crediting each expense account for an amount equal to its own debit balance.

Advertising Expense 520

Date	Explanation	Ref.	Debit	Credit	Balance
20X2					
Apr. 28	Printed advertisements	GJ2	35		35
30	Closing entry	GJ4		35	0

Interest Expense 530

Date	Explanation	Ref.	Debit	Credit	Balance
20X2					
Apr. 30	Accrue interest	GJ2	79		79
30	Closing entry	GJ4		79	0

Supplies Expense 540

Date	Explanation	Ref.	Debit	Credit	Balance
20X2					
Apr. 30	Supplies used	GJ3	25		25
30	Closing entry	GJ4		25	0

Insurance Expense 545

Date	Explanation	Ref.	Debit	Credit	Balance
20X2					
Apr. 30	Expired insurance	GJ3	100		100
30	Closing entry	GJ4		100	0

Depreciation Expense–Equipment 551

Date	Explanation	Ref.	Debit	Credit	Balance
20X2					
Apr. 30	Monthly depreciation	GJ3	35		35
30	Closing entry	GJ4		35	0

Depreciation Expense–Vehicles 556

Date	Explanation	Ref.	Debit	Credit	Balance
20X2					
Apr. 30	Monthly depreciation	GJ3	200		200
30	Closing entry	GJ4		200	0

Closing entry 3: The income summary account's $61 credit balance equals the company's net income for the month of April. To close income summary, debit the account for $61 and credit the owner's capital account for the same amount.

General Journal — GJ4

Date	Account Title and Description	Ref.	Debit	Credit
20X2				
Apr. 30	Income Summary	600	784	
	Wages Expense	500		280
	Gas Expense	510		30
	Advertising Expense	520		35
	Interest Expense	530		79
	Supplies Expense	540		25
	Insurance Expense	545		100
	Depreciation Expense–Equipment	551		35
	Depreciation Expense–Vehicles	556		200
	Close debit-balance accounts			
30	Income Summary	600	61	
	J. Green, Capital	300		61
	Close income summary			

Income Summary — 600

Date	Explanation	Ref.	Debit	Credit	Balance
20X2					
Apr. 30	Credit-balance accounts	GJ3		845	845
30	Debit-balance accounts	GJ4	784		61
30	Transfer to capital	GJ4	61		0

J. Green, Capital — 300

Date	Explanation	Ref.	Debit	Credit	Balance
20X2					
Apr. 1	Owner investment	GJ1		15,000	15,000
30	Net income	GJ4		61	15,061

In partnerships, a compound entry transfers each partner's share of net income or loss to their own capital account. In corporations, income summary is closed to the retained earnings account.

Closing entry 4: Mr. Green's drawing account has a $50 debit balance. To close the account, credit it for $50 and debit the owner's capital account for the same amount.

General Journal · GJ4

Date	Account Title and Description	Ref.	Debit	Credit
30	Income Summary	600	61	
	J. Green, Capital	300		61
	Close income summary			
30	J. Green, Capital	300	50	
	J. Green, Drawing	350		50
	Close drawing account			

J. Green, Capital · 300

Date	Explanation	Ref.	Debit	Credit	Balance
20X2					
Apr. 1	Owner investment	GJ1		15,000	15,000
30	Net income	GJ4		61	15,061
30	Close drawing account	GJ4	50		15,011

J. Green, Drawing · 350

Date	Explanation	Ref.	Debit	Credit	Balance
20X2					
Apr. 29	Owner withdrawal	GJ2	50		50
30	Closing entry	GJ4		50	0

In a partnership, separate entries are made to close each partner's drawing account to his or her own capital account. If a corporation has more than one class of stock and uses dividend accounts to record dividend payments to investors, it usually uses a separate dividend account for each class. If this is the case, the corporation's accounting department makes a compound entry to close each dividend account to the retained earnings account.

The Post-Closing Trial Balance

After the closing entries are journalized and posted, only permanent, balance sheet accounts remain open. A post-closing trial balance is prepared to check the clerical accuracy of the closing entries and to prove that the accounting equation is in balance before the next accounting period begins.

The Greener Landscape Group
Post-Closing Trial Balance
April 30, 20X2

	Account	Debit	Credit
100	Cash	$ 6,355	
110	Accounts Receivable	200	
140	Supplies	25	
145	Prepaid Insurance	1,100	
150	Equipment	3,000	
151	Accumulated Depreciation–Equipment		$ 35
155	Vehicles	15,000	
156	Accumulated Depreciation–Vehicles		200
200	Accounts Payable		50
210	Wages Payable		80
220	Interest Payable		79
250	Unearned Revenue		225
280	Notes Payable		10,000
300	J. Green, Capital		15,011
		$25,680	$25,680

Page 39 explains how to locate errors when the two columns of a trial balance are unequal. Since there are several types of errors that trial balances fail to uncover, however, each closing entry must be journalized and posted carefully.

A Summary of the Accounting Cycle

The accounting cycle begins with the analysis of transactions recorded on source documents such as invoices and checks; it ends with the completion of a post-closing trial balance. This cycle consists of the following steps:

1. Analyze and journalize transactions.

2. Post the journal entries to the general ledger accounts.

3. Prepare a trial balance.

4. Journalize and post the adjusting entries.

5. Prepare an adjusted trial balance.

6. Prepare financial statements.

7. Journalize and post the closing entries.

8. Prepare a post-closing trial balance.

Steps one and two occur as often as needed during an accounting period. Steps three, four, five, and six occur at the end of each accounting period. Steps seven and eight usually occur only at the end of each fiscal year, but these steps may be completed at the end of each accounting period if the company chooses to do so.

If a work sheet is used, steps three, four, and five are initially recorded on the work sheet, which makes it possible to complete step six more quickly, but all adjusting entries on the work sheet must be journalized and posted before closing entries are made.

Reversing Entries

At the beginning of each accounting period, some accountants use **reversing entries** to cancel out the adjusting entries that were made to accrue revenues and expenses at the end of the previous accounting period. Reversing entries make it easier to record subsequent transactions by eliminating the need for certain compound entries.

Suppose Mr. Green makes an adjusting entry at the end of April to account for $80 in unpaid wages. This adjustment involves an $80 debit to the wages expense account and an $80 credit to the wages payable account.

General Journal   GJ2

Date	Account Title and Description	Ref.	Debit	Credit
30	Interest Expense	530	79	
	Interest Payable	220		79
	Accrue interest			
30	Wages Expense	500	80	
	Wages Payable	210		80
	Accrue wages 4-27 to 4-30			

Wages Expense   500

Date	Explanation	Ref.	Debit	Credit	Balance
20X2					
Apr. 26	Wages through 4-26	GJ2	200		200
30	Accrue wages 4-27 to 4-30	GJ2	80		280

Wages Payable   210

Date	Explanation	Ref.	Debit	Credit	Balance
20X2					
Apr. 30	Accrue wages 4-27 to 4-30	GJ2		80	80

If Mr. Green does not reverse the adjusting entry, he must remember that part of May's first payroll payment (for work completed in April) has already been recorded in the wages payable and wages expense accounts. Assuming Mr. Green pays $200 in wages on May 10, he makes a compound entry that decreases (debits) wages payable to $0, increases (debits) wages expense by an amount equal to the wage expenses for May 1 through May 10, and decreases (credits) cash for an amount equal to the total payment.

General Journal   GJ5

Date	Account Title and Description	Ref.	Debit	Credit
20X2				
May 10	Wages Payable	210	80	
	Wages Expense	500	120	
	Cash	100		200
	Wages 4-27 to 5-10			

Wages Payable   210

Date	Explanation	Ref.	Debit	Credit	Balance
20X2					
Apr. 30	Accrue wages 4-27 to 4-30	GJ2		80	80
May 10	Pay accrued wages	GJ5	80		0

Wages Expense   500

Date	Explanation	Ref.	Debit	Credit	Balance
20X2					
Apr. 26	Wages through 4-26	GJ2	200		200
30	Accrue wages 4-27 to 4-30	GJ2	80		280
May 10	Wages 5-1 to 5-10	GJ5	120		400

Cash   100

Date	Explanation	Ref.	Debit	Credit	Balance
9	Paid for servicing mall	GJ4	500		8,000
10	Wages 4-27 to 5-10	GJ5		200	7,800

To avoid the need for a compound entry like the one shown on the previous page, Mr. Green may choose to reverse the April 30 adjustment for accrued wages when the May accounting period begins. The reversing entry decreases (debits) wages payable for $80 and decreases (credits) wages expense for $80.

General Journal — GJ4

Date	Account Title and Description	Ref.	Debit	Credit
20X2				
May 1	Wages Payable	210	80	
	Wages Expense	500		80
	Reverse wage accrual			

Wages Payable — 210

Date	Explanation	Ref.	Debit	Credit	Balance
20X2					
Apr. 30	Accrue wages 4-27 to 4-30	GJ2		80	80
May 1	Reverse accrual	GJ4	80		0

Wages Expense — 500

Date	Explanation	Ref.	Debit	Credit	Balance
20X2					
Apr. 26	Wages through 4-26	GJ2	200		200
30	Accrue wages 4-27 to 4-30	GJ2	80		280
May 1	Reverse accrual	GJ4		80	200

If the reversing entry is made, the May 10 payroll payment can be recorded with a simple entry that increases (debits) wages expense for $200 and decreases (credits) cash for $200.

General Journal — GJ5

Date	Account Title and Description	Ref.	Debit	Credit
20X2				
May 10	Wages Expense	500	200	
	Cash	100		200
	Wages 4-27 to 5-10			

Wages Expense — 500

Date	Explanation	Ref.	Debit	Credit	Balance
20X2					
Apr. 26	Wages through 4-26	GJ2	200		200
30	Accrue wages 4-27 to 4-30	GJ2	80		280
May 1	Reverse accrual	GJ4		80	200
10	Wages 4-27 to 5-10	GJ5	200		400

Cash — 100

Date	Explanation	Ref.	Debit	Credit	Balance
9	Paid for servicing mall	GJ4	500		8,000
10	Wages 4-27 to 5-10	GJ5		200	7,800

Between May 1 when the reversing entry is made and May 10 when the payroll entry is recorded, the company's total liabilities and total expenses are understated. This temporary inaccuracy in the books is acceptable only because financial statements are not prepared during this period.

When the temporary accounts are closed at the end of an accounting period, subsequent reversing entries create abnormal balances in the affected expense and revenue accounts. For example, if the wages expense account is closed on April 30, a reversing entry on May 1 creates a credit balance in the account. The credit balance is offset by the May 10 debit entry, and the account balance then shows current period expenses.

Wages Expense — 500

Date	Explanation	Ref.	Debit	Credit	Balance
20X2					
Apr. 26	Wages through 4-26	GJ2	200		200
30	Accrue wages 4-27 to 4-30	GJ2	80		280
30	Closing entry	GJ4		280	0
May 1	Reverse accrual	GJ4		80	(80)
10	Wages 4-27 to 5-10	GJ5	200		120

Correcting Entries

Accountants must make **correcting entries** when they find errors. There are two ways to make correcting entries: reverse the incorrect entry and then use a second journal entry to record the transaction correctly, or make a single journal entry that, when combined with the original but incorrect entry, fixes the error.

After making a credit purchase for supplies worth $50 on April 5, suppose Mr. Green accidently credits accounts receivable instead of accounts payable.

General Journal — GJ1

Date	Account Title and Description	Ref.	Debit	Credit
Apr. 5	Supplies	140	50	
	Accounts Receivable	110		50
	Bought office supplies			

Mr. Green discovers the error on May 2, after receiving a bill for the supplies. He may use two entries to fix the error: one that reverses the incorrect entry by debiting accounts receivable for $50 and crediting supplies for $50, and another that records the transaction correctly by debiting supplies for $50 and crediting accounts payable for $50.

General Journal   GJ4

Date	Account Title and Description	Ref.	Debit	Credit
May 2	Accounts Receivable	110	50	
	Supplies	140		50
	Reverses April 5 error			
2	Supplies	110	50	
	Accounts Payable	200		50
	Correcting entry for April 5			

Or Mr. Green can fix the error with a single entry that debits accounts receivable for $50 and credits accounts payable for $50.

General Journal   GJ4

Date	Account Title and Description	Ref.	Debit	Credit
May 2	Accounts Receivable	110	50	
	Accounts Payable	200		50
	Corrects April 5 error			

ACCOUNTING FOR A MERCHANDISING COMPANY

Although the accounting cycle and the basic accounting principles are the same for companies that sell merchandise and companies that provide services, merchandising companies use several accounts that service companies do not use. The balance sheet includes an additional current asset called *merchandise inventory*, or simply *inventory*, which records the cost of merchandise held for resale. On balance sheets, the inventory account usually appears just below accounts receivable because inventory is less liquid than accounts receivable.

Music World
Partial Balance Sheet
June 30, 20X3

ASSETS	
Current Assets	
Cash	$10,000
Accounts Receivable	2,000
Inventory	37,000
Supplies	1,000
Prepaid Insurance	2,000
Total Current Assets	$52,000

Merchandising companies also have several specific income statement accounts designed to provide detailed information about revenues and expenses associated with salable merchandise.

Recording Sales

Sales invoices are source documents that provide a record for each sale. For control purposes, sales invoices should be sequentially prenumbered to help the accounting department determine the disposition of every invoice. **Sales revenues** equal the selling price of all products that are sold. In accordance with the revenue recognition

principle, sales revenue is recognized when a customer receives title to the merchandise, regardless of when the money changes hands. If a customer purchases merchandise at a sales counter and takes possession of the goods immediately, the sales invoice or cash register receipt is the only source document needed to record the sale. However, if merchandise is shipped to the customer, a delivery record or shipping document is matched with the invoice to prove that the merchandise has been shipped to the customer.

Suppose a company named Music Suppliers, Inc., sells merchandise worth $1,000 on account to a retail store named Music World. Music Suppliers, Inc., records the sale with the journal entry below.

General Journal					GJ27
Date	Account Title and Description	Ref.	Debit		Credit
20X3					
Jun. 10	Accounts Receivable		1,000		
	Sales				1,000
	Invoice #15932—Music World				

For reference purposes, the journal entry's description often includes the invoice number.

Sales Returns and Allowances

Although sales returns and sales allowances are technically two distinct types of transactions, they are generally recorded in the same account. **Sales returns** occur when customers return defective, damaged, or otherwise undesirable products to the seller. **Sales allowances** occur when customers agree to keep such merchandise in return for a reduction in the selling price.

If Music World returns merchandise worth $100, Music Suppliers, Inc., prepares a **credit memorandum** to account for the return. This credit memorandum becomes the source document for a journal entry that increases (debits) the sales returns and allowances account and decreases (credits) accounts receivable.

General Journal				GJ28
Date	Account Title and Description	Ref.	Debit	Credit
20X3				
Jun. 15	Sales Returns & Allowances		100	
	Accounts Receivable			100
	CM #1243—Music World			

A $100 allowance requires the same entry.

In the sales revenue section of an income statement, the sales returns and allowances account is subtracted from sales because these accounts have the opposite effect on net income. Therefore, sales returns and allowances is considered a **contra-revenue account,** which normally has a debit balance. Recording sales returns and allowances in a separate contra-revenue account allows management to monitor returns and allowances as a percentage of overall sales. High return levels may indicate the presence of serious but correctable problems. For example, improved packaging might minimize damage during shipment, new suppliers might reduce the amount of defective merchandise, or better methods for recording and packaging orders might eliminate or reduce incorrect merchandise shipments. The first step in identifying such problems is to carefully monitor sales returns and allowances in a separate, contra-revenue account.

Sales Discounts

A **sales discount** is an incentive the seller offers in exchange for prompt payment on credit sales. Sales discounts are recorded in another contra-revenue account, enabling management to monitor the effectiveness of the company's discount policy. Invoices generally include **credit terms,** which specify when the customer must pay and define the sales discount if one is available. For example, the credit terms on the invoice below are 2/10, n/30, which is read "two-ten, net thirty."

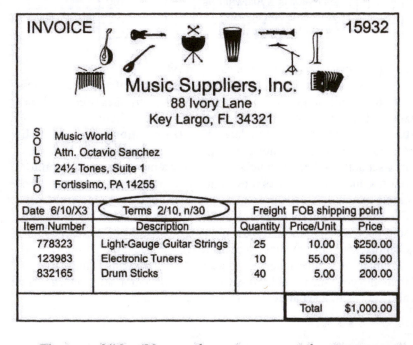

INVOICE 15932

Music Suppliers, Inc.
88 Ivory Lane
Key Largo, FL 34321

SOLD TO
Music World
Attn. Octavio Sanchez
24½ Tones, Suite 1
Fortissimo, PA 14255

Date 6/10/X3	Terms 2/10, n/30		Freight FOB shipping point		
Item Number	Description	Quantity	Price/Unit		Price
778323	Light-Gauge Guitar Strings	25	10.00		$250.00
123983	Electronic Tuners	10	55.00		550.00
832165	Drum Sticks	40	5.00		200.00
				Total	$1,000.00

The terms 2/10, n/30 mean the customer may take a two percent discount on the outstanding balance (original invoice amount less any returns and allowances) if payment occurs within ten days of the invoice date. If the customer chooses not to take the discount, the outstanding balance is due within thirty days. An abbreviation that sometimes appears in the credit terms section of an invoice is *EOM,*

which stands for *end of month*. The terms n/15 EOM indicate that the outstanding balance is due fifteen days after the end of the month in which the invoice is dated.

If Music World returns merchandise worth $100 after receiving a $1,000 order, they still owe Music Suppliers, Inc., $900. Assuming the credit terms are 2/10, n/30 and Music World pays the invoice within ten days, the payment equals $882, an amount calculated by subtracting $18 (2% of $900) from the outstanding balance. To record this payment from Music World, Music Suppliers, Inc., makes a compound journal entry that increases (debits) cash for $882, increases (debits) sales discounts for $18, and decreases (credits) accounts receivable for $900.

	General Journal				GJ29
Date	Account Title and Description	Ref.	Debit	Credit	
20X3					
Jun. 20	Cash		882		
	Sales Discounts		18		
	Accounts Receivable			900	
	Payment for invoice #15932				

Net Sales

Net sales is calculated by subtracting sales returns and allowances and sales discounts from sales. Suppose Music Suppliers, Inc., sells merchandise worth $116,500 during June and, in conjunction with these sales, handles $9,300 in returns and allowances and $1,200 in sales discounts. The company's net sales for June equal $106,000.

Music Suppliers, Inc.
Calculation of Net Sales
For the Month Ended June 30, 20X3

Sales		$116,500
Less: Sales Returns and Allowances	$9,300	
Sales Discounts	1,200	10,500
Net Sales		$106,000

Inventory Systems

There are two systems to account for inventory: the perpetual system and the periodic system. With the **perpetual system,** the inventory account is updated after every inventory purchase or sale. Before computers became widely available, only companies that sold a relatively small number of high-priced items used this system. A complete description of the perpetual system appears later, in the chapter on inventories. The examples in this chapter illustrate the periodic system. Under the **periodic system,** a careful evaluation of inventory occurs only at the end of each accounting period. At that time, each product available for sale is counted and multiplied by its per unit cost, and the total of all such calculations equals the value of inventory.

Recording Purchases

Under the periodic system, a temporary expense account named *merchandise purchases,* or simply *purchases,* is used to record the purchase of goods intended for resale. The source documents used to journalize merchandise purchases include the seller's invoice, the company's purchase order, and a receiving report that verifies the accuracy of the inventory quantities. When Music World receives a shipment of merchandise worth $1,000 on account from Music Suppliers, Inc., Music World increases (debits) the purchases account for $1,000 and increases (credits) accounts payable for $1,000.

	General Journal			GJ16

Date	Account Title and Description	Ref.	Debit	Credit
20X3				
Jun. 10	Purchases		1,000	
	Accounts Payable			1,000
	Invoice #15932—Music Suppliers			

For reference purposes, the journal entry's description usually includes the invoice number.

When a seller pays to ship merchandise to a purchaser, the seller records the cost as a delivery expense, which is considered an operating expense and, more specifically, a selling expense. When a purchaser pays the shipping fees, the purchaser considers the fees to be part of the cost of the merchandise. Instead of recording such fees directly in the purchases account, however, they are recorded in a separate expense account named *freight-in* or *transportation-in*, which provides management with a way to monitor these shipping costs.

If Music World pays a shipping company $30 for delivering the merchandise from Music Suppliers, Inc., Music World increases (debits) freight-in for $30 and decreases (credits) cash for $30.

General Journal				GJ17
Date	Account Title and Description	Ref.	Debit	Credit
20X3				
Jun. 12	Freight-in		30	
	Cash			30
	Shipping fees—invoice #15932			

Freight terms, which indicate whether the purchaser or seller pays the shipping fees, are often specified with the abbreviations FOB shipping point or FOB destination. *FOB* means *free on board.* **FOB shipping point** means the purchaser pays the shipping fees and gains title to the merchandise at the shipping point (the seller's place of business). **FOB destination** means the seller pays the shipping fees and maintains title until the merchandise reaches its destination (the purchaser's place of business).

Purchases Returns and Allowances

When a purchaser receives defective, damaged, or otherwise undesirable merchandise, the purchaser prepares a **debit memorandum** that identifies the items in question and the cost of those items. The purchaser uses the debit memorandum to inform the seller about the return and to prepare a journal entry that decreases (debits) accounts payable and increases (credits) an account named *purchases returns and*

allowances, which is a contra-expense account. Contra-expense accounts normally have credit balances. On the income statement, the purchases returns and allowances account is subtracted from purchases.

If Music World discovers $100 worth of defective merchandise in the shipment from Music Suppliers, Inc., Music World prepares a debit memorandum, returns the merchandise, and makes a journal entry that decreases (debits) accounts payable for $100 and that increases (credits) purchases returns and allowances for $100.

General Journal					GJ19
Date	Account Title and Description	Ref.	Debit	Credit
20X3				
Jun. 15	Accounts Payable		100	
	Purchases Returns & Allowances			100
	DM #1072, Invoice #15932			

For reference purposes, the journal entry's description may include the debit memorandum number and the seller's invoice number.

Purchases Discounts

Companies that take advantage of sales discounts usually record them in an account named *purchases discounts,* which is another contra-expense account that is subtracted from purchases on the income statement. If Music Suppliers, Inc., offers the terms 2/10, n/30 and Music World pays the invoice's outstanding balance of $900 within ten days, Music World takes an $18 discount. To record this payment to Music Suppliers, Inc., Music World makes a compound journal entry that decreases (debits) accounts payable for $900, decreases (credits) cash for $882, and increases (credits) purchases discounts for $18.

General Journal					GJ20
Date	Account Title and Description	Ref.	Debit	Credit
20X3				
Jun. 20	Accounts Payable		900	
	Cash			882
	Purchases Discounts			18
	Paid invoice #15932			

Net Purchases and the Cost of Goods Purchased

Net purchases is found by subtracting the credit balances in the purchases returns and allowances and purchases discounts accounts from the debit balance in the purchases account. The **cost of goods purchased** equals net purchases plus the freight-in account's debit balance.

> Purchases
> − Purchases Returns and Allowances
> − Purchases Discounts
> Net Purchases
> + Freight-in
> = Cost of Goods Purchased

The Cost of Goods Available for Sale and the Cost of Goods Sold

The **cost of goods available for sale** equals the beginning value of inventory plus the cost of goods purchased. The **cost of goods sold** equals the cost of goods available for sale less the ending value of inventory.

> Beginning Inventory
> + Cost of Goods Purchased
> Cost of Goods Available for Sale
> − Ending Inventory
> = Cost of Goods Sold

Gross Profit

Gross profit, which is also called **gross margin,** represents the company's profit from selling merchandise before deducting operating expenses such as salaries, rent, and delivery expenses. Gross profit equals net sales minus the cost of goods sold.

$$
\begin{array}{l}
\text{Net Sales} \\
- \text{ Cost of Goods Sold} \\
\hline
= \text{ Gross Profit}
\end{array}
$$

Financial Statements for a Merchandising Company

The statement of owner's equity and the statement of cash flows are the same for merchandising and service companies. Except for the inventory account, the balance sheet is also the same. But a merchandising company's income statement includes categories that service enterprises do not use. A single-step income statement for a merchandising company lists net sales under revenues and the cost of goods sold under expenses.

Music World
Income Statement
For the Year Ended June 30, 20X3

Revenues		
Net Sales		$1,172,000
Interest Income		7,500
Gain on Sale of Equipment		1,500
Total Revenues		1,181,000
Expenses		
Cost of Goods Sold	$596,600	
Selling Expenses	177,000	
General and Administrative Expenses	152,900	
Interest Expense	18,000	
Total Expenses		944,500
Net Income		$ 236,500

Although the single-step format is easier to read than the multiple-step format, most companies produce a multiple-step income statement, which clearly identifies each step in the calculation of net income or net loss.

Music World
Income Statement
For the Year Ended June 30, 20X3

Sales Revenues			
Sales			$1,240,000
Less: Sales Returns and Allowances		$ 65,000	
Sales Discounts		3,000	68,000
Net Sales			1,172,000
Cost of Goods Sold			
Inventory, July 1, 20X2		37,000	
Purchases	$610,000		
Less: Purchases Returns and Allowances	$9,000		
Purchases Discounts	8,000	17,000	
Net Purchases		593,000	
Add: Freight-in		5,600	
Cost of Goods Purchased		598,600	
Cost of Goods Available for Sale		635,600	
Less: Inventory, June 30, 20X3		39,000	
Cost of Goods Sold			596,600
Gross Profit			575,400
Operating Expenses			
Selling Expenses			
Sales Salaries Expense	120,000		
Sales Commission Expense	21,000		
Delivery Expense	15,000		
Store Rent Expense	12,000		
Depreciation Expense–Store Equipment	9,000		
Total Selling Expenses		177,000	
General and Administrative Expenses			
Office Salaries Expense	140,000		
Insurance Expense	6,000		
Depreciation Expense–Office Equipment	5,000		
Office Rent Expense	1,200		
Office Supplies Expense	700		
Total General and Administrative Expenses		152,900	
Total Operating Expenses			329,900
Operating Income			245,500
Other Income/(Expense), Net			
Interest Income		7,500	
Gain on Sale of Equipment		1,500	
Interest Expense		(18,000)	
Other Income/(Expense), Net			(9,000)
Net Income			$ 236,500

Adjusting the Inventory Account

Under the periodic system of accounting for inventory, the inventory account's balance remains unchanged throughout the accounting period and must be updated after a physical count determines the value of inventory at the end of the accounting period. The inventory account's balance may be updated with adjusting entries or as part of the closing entry process. When adjusting entries are used, two separate entries are made. The first adjusting entry clears the inventory account's beginning balance by debiting income summary and crediting inventory for an amount equal to the beginning inventory balance.

General Journal — GJ21

Date	Account Title and Description	Ref.	Debit	Credit
20X3				
Jun. 30	Income Summary	600	37,000	
	Inventory	125		37,000
	Adjust beginning inventory			

Income Summary — 600

Date	Explanation	Ref.	Debit	Credit	Balance
20X3					
Jun. 30	Beginning inventory	GJ21	37,000		(37,000)

Inventory — 125

Date	Explanation	Ref.	Debit	Credit	Balance
20X2					
Jul. 1	Beginning Inventory	GJ1	37,000		37,000
20X3					
Jun. 30	Beginning inventory	GJ21		37,000	0

The second adjusting entry debits inventory and credits income summary for the value of inventory at the end of the accounting period.

General Journal — GJ21

Date	Account Title and Description	Ref.	Debit	Credit
20X3				
Jun. 30	Income Summary	600	37,000	
	Inventory	125		37,000
	Adjust beginning inventory			
30	Inventory	125	39,000	
	Income Summary	600		39,000
	Adjust ending inventory			

Inventory — 125

Date	Explanation	Ref.	Debit	Credit	Balance
20X2					
Jul. 1	Beginning Inventory	GJ1	37,000		37,000
20X3					
Jun. 30	Beginning inventory	GJ21		37,000	0
30	Ending inventory	GJ21	39,000		39,000

Income Summary — 600

Date	Explanation	Ref.	Debit	Credit	Balance
20X3					
Jun. 30	Beginning inventory	GJ21	37,000		(37,000)
30	Ending inventory	GJ21		39,000	2,000

Combined, these two adjusting entries update the inventory account's balance and, until closing entries are made, leave income summary with a balance that reflects the increase or decrease in inventory.

ACCOUNTING FOR A
MERCHANDISING
COMPANY

Inventory Adjustments on the Work Sheet

On a work sheet, the beginning inventory balance in the trial balance columns combines with the two inventory adjustments to produce the ending inventory balance in the adjusted trial balance columns. This balance carries across to the work sheet's balance sheet columns.

Account	Trial Balance		Adjustments		Adjusted Trial Balance		Income Statement		Balance Sheet	
	Dr.	Cr.	Dr.	Cr.	Dr.	Cr.	Dr.	Cr.	Dr.	Cr.
Inventory	37,000		39,000	37,000	39,000				39,000	

Income summary, which appears on the work sheet whenever adjusting entries are used to update inventory, is always placed at the bottom of the work sheet's list of accounts. The two adjustments to income summary receive special treatment on the work sheet. Instead of combining the adjustments and placing the result in one of the adjusted trial balance columns, both adjustments are transferred to the adjusted trial balance columns and then to the income statement columns. Income summary's debit entry on the work sheet is used to report the beginning inventory balance on the income statement, and income summary's credit entry is used to report the ending inventory balance on the income statement. Each of these amounts is needed to calculate cost of goods sold.

Account	Trial Balance		Adjustments		Adjusted Trial Balance		Income Statement		Balance Sheet	
	Dr.	Cr.	Dr.	Cr.	Dr.	Cr.	Dr.	Cr.	Dr.	Cr.
Income Summary			37,000	39,000	37,000	39,000	37,000	39,000		

Closing Entries for a Merchandising Company

Although merchandising and service companies use the same four closing entries, merchandising companies usually have more temporary accounts to close. The additional accounts include sales, sales returns and allowances, sales discounts, purchases, purchases returns and allowances, purchases discounts, and freight-in. Consider Music World's four closing entries.

1. Close all income statement accounts with credit balances to the income summary account. The entry shown below assumes the inventory account was updated with adjusting entries and, therefore, does not include it.

General Journal   GJ22

Date	Account Title and Description	Ref.	Debit	Credit
20X3				
Jun. 30	Sales	400	1,240,000	
	Purchases Returns & Allowances	501	9,000	
	Purchases Discounts	502	8,000	
	Interest Income	420	7,500	
	Gain on Sale of Equipment	430	1,500	
	Income Summary	600		1,266,000
	Close credit-balance accounts			

Accountants who choose to update the inventory account during the closing process instead of with adjusting entries include the *ending* inventory balance with this first closing entry.

General Journal   GJ22

Date	Account Title and Description	Ref.	Debit	Credit
20X3				
Jun. 30	Inventory	125	39,000	
	Sales	400	1,240,000	
	Purchases Returns & Allowances	501	9,000	
	Purchases Discounts	502	8,000	
	Interest Income	420	7,500	
	Gain on Sale of Equipment	430	1,500	
	Income Summary	600		1,305,000
	Close credit-balance accounts			

Notice how this entry has the same effect on the accounts as the closing entry at the top of this page combined with the second of the two adjusting entries discussed on pages 96 and 97.

2. Close all income statement accounts with debit balances to the income summary account. The entry shown below assumes the inventory account was updated with adjusting entries and, therefore, does not include it.

General Journal — GJ22

Date	Account Title and Description	Ref.	Debit	Credit
20X3				
Jun. 30	Income Summary	600	1,031,500	
	Sales Returns and Allowances	401		65,000
	Sales Discounts	402		3,000
	Purchases	500		610,000
	Freight-in	510		5,600
	Depreciation Expense–Store Equipment	550		9,000
	Sales Salaries Expense	520		120,000
	Sales Commission Expense	525		21,000
	Store Rent Expense	530		12,000
	Delivery Expense	540		15,000
	Depreciation Expense–Office Equipment	555		5,000
	Office Salaries Expense	521		140,000
	Insurance Expense	560		6,000
	Office Rent Expense	531		1,200
	Office Supplies Expense	545		700
	Interest Expense	570		18,000
	Close debit-balance accounts			

If the inventory account is updated during the closing entry process, this closing entry includes a credit equal to the beginning inventory balance ($37,000), which increases the debit to income summary by a corresponding amount (to $1,068,500).

At this point, income summary has the same balance whether adjusting or closing entries are used to update inventory. If adjusting entries are used, four separate entries contribute to the income summary account's balance.

Income Summary — 600

Date	Explanation	Ref.	Debit	Credit	Balance
20X3					
Jun. 30	Beginning inventory	GJ21	37,000		(37,000)
30	Ending inventory	GJ21		39,000	2,000
30	Credit-balance accounts	GJ22		1,266,000	1,268,000
30	Debit-balance accounts	GJ22	1,031,500		236,500

If closing entries are used to update inventory, the first two closing entries establish the income summary account's balance.

Income Summary   600

Date	Explanation	Ref.	Debit	Credit	Balance
20X3					
Jun. 30	Credit-balance accounts	GJ22		1,305,000	1,305,000
30	Debit-balance accounts	GJ22	1,068,500		236,500

The income summary account now has a balance equal to the company's net income or net loss.

3. Close income summary to the owner's capital account.

General Journal   GJ22

Date	Account Title and Description	Ref.	Debit	Credit
20X3				
Jun. 30	Income Summary	600	236,500	
	Octavio Sanchez, Capital	300		236,500
	Close income summary			

4. Close the owner's drawing account to the owner's capital account. Assume the owner's drawing account has a $40,000 balance.

General Journal   GJ22

Date	Account Title and Description	Ref.	Debit	Credit
20X3				
Jun. 30	Octavio Sanchez, Capital	600	40,000	
	Octavio Sanchez, Drawing	300		40,000
	Close drawing account			

The Work Sheet When Closing Entries Update Inventory

If closing entries are used to update inventory, no adjusting entries affect the inventory account, so the beginning inventory balance appears in the work sheet's trial balance and adjusted trial balance columns. This beginning inventory balance is first extended to the income statement debit column. Then, the value of inventory at the end of the accounting period is placed in the work sheet's income statement credit column and balance sheet debit column.

Account	Trial Balance		Adjustments		Adjusted Trial Balance		Income Statement		Balance Sheet	
	Dr.	Cr.	Dr.	Cr.	Dr.	Cr.	Dr.	Cr.	Dr.	Cr.
Inventory	37,000				37,000		37,000	39,000	39,000	

The entries in the work sheet's income statement columns are used in the calculation of cost of goods sold on the income statement, and the entry in the work sheet's balance sheet debit column provides the correct balance for merchandise inventory on the balance sheet.

Subsidiary Ledgers

A **subsidiary ledger** is a group of similar accounts whose combined balances equal the balance in a specific general ledger account. The general ledger account that summarizes a subsidiary ledger's account balances is called a **control account** or **master account**. For example, an accounts receivable subsidiary ledger (customers' subsidiary ledger) includes a separate account for each customer who makes credit purchases. The combined balance of every account in this subsidiary ledger equals the balance of accounts receivable in the general ledger. Posting a debit or credit to a subsidiary ledger account and also to a general ledger control account does not violate the rule that total

Accounts Receivable Subsidiary Ledger

C. Daley — AR1

Date	Ref.	Debit	Credit	Balance
20X1				
Mar. 18		200		200

B. Johnson — AR2

Date	Ref.	Debit	Credit	Balance
20X1				
Mar. 22		700		700

L. Jones — AR3

Date	Ref.	Debit	Credit	Balance
20X1				
Mar. 15		500		500

P. O'Reilly — AR4

Date	Ref.	Debit	Credit	Balance
20X1				
Mar. 5		1,500		1,500
Mar. 29		1,000		2,500

T. Smith — AR5

Date	Ref.	Debit	Credit	Balance
20X1				
Mar. 1		1,000		1,000

Control Account

Accounts Receivable — 110

Date	Ref.	Debit	Credit	Balance
20X1				
Mar. 31		4,900		4,900

```
   200
   700
   500
 2,500
+1,000
 4,900
```

Here and throughout most of this chapter, each account's explanation column is removed to save space.

debit and credit entries must balance because subsidiary ledger accounts are not part of the general ledger; they are supplemental accounts that provide the detail to support the balance in a control account.

The accounts receivable subsidiary ledger is essential to most businesses. Companies may have hundreds or even thousands of customers who purchase items on credit, who make one or more payments for those items, and who sometimes return items or purchase additional items before they finish paying for prior purchases. Recording all credit purchases, returns, and subsequent payments in a single account would make an individual customer's balance virtually impossible to calculate because the customer's transactions would be interspersed among thousands of other transactions. But the accounts receivable subsidiary ledger provides quick access to each customer's balance and account activity.

Companies create subsidiary ledgers whenever they need to monitor the individual components of a controlling general ledger account. In addition to the accounts receivable subsidiary ledger, companies often use an accounts payable subsidiary ledger (creditors' subsidiary ledger), which has separate accounts for each creditor, an inventory subsidiary ledger, which has separate accounts for each product, and a property, plant, and equipment subsidiary ledger, which has separate accounts for each long-lived asset.

Selected General Ledger Accounts

Cash	Accounts Receivable	Inventory	Property, Plant, and Equipment	Accounts Payable	Capital
9,000	1,000	1,000	140,000	1,000	50,000

Adams		Bolts		Building		Acme	
450		200		99,000			500
Baker		Nuts		Car		Boltz-It	
100		200		11,000			100
Cook		Pipes		Computer		Nuts! Inc.	
200		300		2,500			100
Davis		Screws		Desk		Screwy Al's	
50		100		500			50
Evans		Washers		Truck		We Sell It	
200		200		27,000			250

Accounts Receivable Subsidiary Ledger | Inventory Subsidiary Ledger | Property, Plant, and Equipment Subsidiary Ledger | Accounts Payable Subsidiary Ledger

Special Journals

Entering transactions in the general journal and posting them to the correct general ledger accounts is time consuming. In the general journal, a simple transaction requires three lines—two to list the accounts and one to describe the transaction. The transaction must then be posted to each general ledger account. If the transaction affects a control account, the posting must be done twice—once to the subsidiary ledger account and once to the controlling general ledger account. To speed up this process, companies use special journals to record repetitive transactions that affect the same set of accounts and have a consistent description. Such transactions can be documented on one line in a special journal. Then, instead of separately posting individual entries, each column's total is posted at the end of the accounting period.

Although companies create special journals for other types of repetitive transactions, almost all merchandising companies use special journals for sales, purchases, cash receipts, and cash disbursements.

Sales Journal · S1

Date	Invoice	Customer	Ref.	Dr. Accounts Receivable Cr. Sales

- Used for all sales of merchandise on account.
- Each entry debits accounts receivable and credits sales.

Purchases Journal · P1

Date	Supplier	Ref.	Dr. Purchases Cr. Accounts Payable

- Used for all purchases of merchandise on account.
- Each entry debits purchases and credits accounts payable.

Cash Receipts Journal · CR1

Date	Account	Ref.	Cash Dr.	Sales Discounts Dr.	Accounts Receivable Cr.	Sales Cr.	Other Cr.

- Used for all cash receipts.
- Each entry includes a debit to cash and has equal debits and credits.

Cash Disbursements Journal · CD1

Date	Check	Account	Ref.	Accounts Payable Dr.	Other Dr.	Purchases Discounts Cr.	Cash Cr.

- Used for all cash payments.
- Each entry includes a credit to cash and has equal debits and credits.

Sales journal. The sales journal lists all credit sales made to customers. Sales returns and cash sales are not recorded in this journal. Entries in the sales journal typically include the date, invoice number, customer name, and amount. Invoices are the source documents that provide this information. In its most basic form, a sales journal has only one column for recording transaction amounts. Each entry increases (debits) accounts receivable and increases (credits) sales.

Notice the dates and posting references applied to each entry in the illustration to the right. Each day, individual sales journal entries are posted to the accounts receivable subsidiary ledger accounts so that customer balances remain current. Customer account numbers (or check marks if customer accounts are simply kept in alphabetical order) are placed in the sales journal's reference column to indicate that the entries have been posted. At the end of the accounting period, the column total is posted to the accounts receivable and sales accounts in the general ledger. Account numbers are placed in parentheses below the column to indicate that the total has been posted.

Many companies use a multi-column (columnar) sales journal that provides separate columns for specific sales accounts and for sales tax payable. Each line in a multi-column journal must contain equal debits and credits. For example, the entries in the sales journal to the right appear below in a multi-column sales journal that tracks hardware sales, plumbing sales, wire sales, and sales tax payable. Individual entries are still posted daily to the accounts receivable subsidiary ledger accounts, and each column total is posted at the end of the accounting period to the appropriate general ledger account.

Sales Journal　　　　　　　　　　　　　　　　S1

Date	Invoice	Customer Account Debited	Ref.	Accounts Receivable Dr.	Hardware Sales Cr.	Plumbing Sales Cr.	Wire Sales Cr.	Sales Tax Payable Cr.
20X1								
Mar. 1	1561	Smith	AR5	1,000	200	700	40	60
Mar. 5	1562	O'Reilly	AR4	1,500	1,000	410		90
Mar. 15	1563	Jones	AR3	500			470	30
Mar. 18	1564	Daley	AR1	200			188	12
Mar. 22	1565	Johnson	AR2	700	358	300		42
Mar. 29	1566	O'Reilly	AR4	1,000	940			60
Totals				4,900	2,498	1,410	698	294
				(110)	(410)	(420)	(430)	(290)

Sales Journal   S1

Date	Invoice	Customer Account Debited	Ref.	Dr. Accounts Recievable Cr. Sales
20X1				
Mar. 1	1561	T. Smith	AR5	1,000
Mar. 5	1562	P. O'Reilly	AR4	1,500
Mar. 15	1563	L. Jones	AR3	500
Mar. 18	1564	C. Daley	AR1	200
Mar. 22	1565	B. Johnson	AR2	700
Mar. 29	1566	P. O'Reilly	AR4	1,000
Totals				4,900
				(110) (400)

Individual entries are posted daily to the accounts receivable subsidiary ledger accounts.

The column total is posted at the end of the period to the general ledger accounts.

C. Daley   AR1

Date	Ref.	Debit	Credit	Balance
20X1				
Mar. 18	S1	200		200

Accounts Receivable   110

Date	Ref.	Debit	Credit	Balance
20X1				
Mar. 31	S1	4,900		4,900

B. Johnson   AR2

Date	Ref.	Debit	Credit	Balance
20X1				
Mar. 22	S1	700		700

Sales   400

Date	Ref.	Debit	Credit	Balance
20X1				
Mar. 31	S1		4,900	4,900

L. Jones   AR3

Date	Ref.	Debit	Credit	Balance
20X1				
Mar. 15	S1	500		500

P. O'Reilly   AR4

Date	Ref.	Debit	Credit	Balance
20X1				
Mar. 5	S1	1,500		1,500
Mar. 29	S1	1,000		2,500

T. Smith   AR5

Date	Ref.	Debit	Credit	Balance
20X1				
Mar. 1	S1	1,000		1,000

Purchases journal. The purchases journal lists all credit purchases of merchandise. Entries in this journal usually include the date of the entry, the name of the supplier, and the amount of the transaction. Some companies include columns to identify the invoice date and credit terms, thereby making the purchases journal a tool that helps the companies take advantage of discounts just before they expire. The purchases journal to the right has only one column for recording transaction amounts. Each entry increases (debits) purchases and increases (credits) accounts payable.

Each day, individual entries are posted to the accounts payable subsidiary ledger accounts. Creditor account numbers (or check marks if the creditor accounts are not numbered) are placed in the purchases journal's reference column to indicate that the entries have been posted. At the end of the accounting period, the column total is posted to purchases and accounts payable in the general ledger. Account numbers are placed in parentheses below the column to indicate that the total has been posted.

Companies that frequently make credit purchases of items other than merchandise use a multi-column purchases journal. For example, the purchases journal below includes columns for supplies and equipment. Of course, every purchase in the journal below must credit accounts payable; equipment purchased with a note payable or supplies purchased with cash would not be recorded in this journal. Individual entries are still posted daily to the accounts payable subsidiary ledger accounts, and each column total is posted at the end of the accounting period to the appropriate general ledger account.

Purchases Journal   P1

Date	Supplier Account Creditied	Ref.	Purchases Dr.	Supplies Dr.	Equipment Dr.	Accounts Payable Cr.
20X1						
Mar. 2	Dandy One	AP1	800			800
Mar. 7	Supply House	AP6		200		200
Mar. 12	Smith Brothers	AP3	900			900
Mar. 18	Peters & Jones	AP2	600			600
Mar. 23	Equipment Hut	AP5			2,500	2,500
Mar. 28	Woody Blues	AP4	1,400			1,400
Totals			3,700	200	2,500	6,400
			(500)	(140)	(150)	(200)

Purchases Journal P1

Date	Supplier Account Credited	Invoice Date	Terms	Ref.	Dr. Purchases Cr. Accounts Payable
20X1					
Mar. 2	Dandy One	Mar. 1	n/30	AP1	800
Mar. 12	Smith Brothers	Mar. 10	2/10 n/30	AP3	900
Mar. 18	Peters & Jones	Mar. 18	1/15 n/30	AP2	600
Mar. 28	Woody Blues	Mar. 28	n/10 EOM	AP4	1,400
Totals					3,700
					(500) (200)

Individual entries are posted daily to the accounts payable subsidiary ledger accounts.

The column total is posted at the end of the period to the general ledger accounts.

Dandy One AP1

Date	Ref.	Debit	Credit	Balance
20X1				
Mar. 2	P1		800	800

Peters & Jones AP2

Date	Ref.	Debit	Credit	Balance
20X1				
Mar. 18	P1		600	600

Smith Brothers AP3

Date	Ref.	Debit	Credit	Balance
20X1				
Mar. 12	P1		900	900

Woody Blues AP4

Date	Ref.	Debit	Credit	Balance
20X1				
Mar. 28	P1		1,400	1,400

Purchases 500

Date	Ref.	Debit	Credit	Balance
20X1				
Mar. 31	P1	3,700		3,700

Accounts Payable 200

Date	Ref.	Debit	Credit	Balance
20X1				
Mar. 31	P1		3,700	3,700

Cash receipts journal. Transactions that increase cash are recorded in a multi-column cash receipts journal. If sales discounts are offered to customers, the journal includes a separate debit column for sales discounts. Credit columns for accounts receivable and for sales are normally present, but companies that frequently receive cash from other, specific sources use additional columns to record those types of cash receipts. In addition, the cash receipts journal includes a column named *Other,* which is used to record various types of cash receipts that occur infrequently and therefore do not warrant a separate column. For example, cash receipts from capital investments, bank loans, and interest revenues are generally recorded in the *Other* column. However, a company that provides consumer loans and receives interest payments from many customers would probably include a separate column for interest revenue. Whenever a credit entry affects accounts receivable or appears in the *Other* column, the specific account is identified in the column named *Account.*

Accounts receivable payments are posted daily to the individual subsidiary ledger accounts, and customer account numbers (or check marks if the customer accounts are not numbered) are placed in the cash receipts journal's reference column. At the end of the accounting period, each column total is posted to the general ledger account listed at the top of the column, and the account number is placed in parentheses below the total. Entries in the *Other* column are posted individually to the general ledger accounts affected, and the account numbers are placed in the cash receipts journal's reference column. A capital *X* is placed below the *Other* column to indicate that the column total cannot be posted to a general ledger account.

Cash Receipts Journal — CR1

Date	Account	Ref.	Cash Dr.	Sales Discounts Dr.	Accounts Receivable Cr.	Sales Cr.	Other Cr.
20X1							
Mar. 2	Gander, Capital	300	5,000				5,000
Mar. 7			2,500			2,500	
Mar. 11	T. Smith	AR5	794	16	800		
Mar. 14			2,800			2,800	
Mar. 21			2,100			2,100	
Mar. 25	L. Jones	AR3	490	10	500		
Mar. 28			2,400			2,400	
Mar. 31	P. O'Reilly	AR4	1,500		1,500		
Mar. 31	Interest Income	420	100				100
Totals			17,674	26	2,800	9,800	5,100
			(100)	(402)	(110)	(400)	X

➤ Entries that affect control accounts are posted daily to the subsidiary ledger accounts.

➤ Column totals (besides *Other*) are posted at the end of the period to the general ledger accounts.

L. Jones — AR3

Date	Ref.	Debit	Credit	Balance
20X1				
Mar. 15	S1	500		500
Mar. 25	CR1		500	0

Cash — 100

Date	Ref.	Debit	Credit	Balance
20X1				
Mar. 31	CR1	17,674		17,674

Accounts Receivable — 110

Date	Ref.	Debit	Credit	Balance
20X1				
Mar. 31	S1	4,900		4,900
Mar. 31	CR1		2,800	2,100

P. O'Reilly — AR4

Date	Ref.	Debit	Credit	Balance
20X1				
Mar. 5	S1	1,500		1,500
Mar. 29	S1	1,000		2,500
Mar. 31	CR1		1,500	1,000

Sales — 400

Date	Ref.	Debit	Credit	Balance
20X1				
Mar. 31	S1		4,900	4,900
Mar. 31	CR1		9,800	14,700

T. Smith — AR5

Date	Ref.	Debit	Credit	Balance
20X1				
Mar. 1	S1	1,000		1,000
Mar. 5	GJ1		200	800
Mar. 11	CR1		800	0

Sales Discounts — 402

Date	Ref.	Debit	Credit	Balance
20X1				
Mar. 31	CR1	26		26

Entries in the *Other* column are posted individually to the general ledger accounts.

Gander, Capital — 300

Date	Ref.	Debit	Credit	Balance
20X1				
Mar. 2	CR1		5,000	1,200

Interest Income — 420

Date	Ref.	Debit	Credit	Balance
20X1				
Mar. 31	CR1		100	100

Cash disbursements journal. Transactions that decrease cash are recorded in the cash disbursements journal. The cash disbursements journal to the right has one debit column for accounts payable and another debit column for all other types of cash payment transactions. It has credit columns for purchases discounts and for cash. Since each entry debits a control account (accounts payable) or an account listed in the column named *Other,* the specific account being debited must be identified on every line.

The nature of each company's transactions determines which columns this journal includes. For example, companies sometimes choose to include separate debit columns for regularly used accounts such as salaries expense, sales commissions expense, or other specific accounts affected by cash disbursements.

Entries that affect accounts payable are posted daily to the individual subsidiary ledger accounts, and creditor account numbers (or check marks if the creditor accounts are not numbered) are placed in the cash disbursements journal's reference column. At the end of the accounting period, each column total is posted to the general ledger account listed at the top of the column, and the account number is placed in parentheses below the total. Entries in the *Other* column are posted individually to the general ledger accounts affected, and the account numbers are placed in the cash disbursements journal's reference column. A capital X is placed below the *Other* column to indicate that the column total cannot be posted to a general ledger account.

Cash Disbursements Journal — CD1

Date	Check	Account	Ref.	Accounts Payable Dr.	Other Dr.	Purchases Discounts Cr.	Cash Cr.
20X1							
Mar. 1	1973	Rent Expense	540		1,200		1,200
Mar. 10	1974	Utilities Expense	550		400		400
Mar. 15	1975	Supplies	170		250		250
Mar. 20	1976	Smith Brothers	AP3	900		18	882
Mar. 31	1977	Dandy One	AP1	800			1,000
Totals				1,700	1,850	18	3,732
				(200)	X	(502)	(100)

Entries that affect control accounts are posted daily to the subsidiary ledger accounts.

Column totals (besides *Other*) are posted at the end of the period to the general ledger accounts.

Dandy One — AP1

Date	Ref.	Debit	Credit	Balance
20X1				
Mar. 2	P1		800	800
Mar. 31	CD1	800		0

Cash — 100

Date	Ref.	Debit	Credit	Balance
20X1				
Mar. 31	CR1	17,674		17,674
Mar. 31	CD1		3,732	13,942

Smith Brothers — AP3

Date	Ref.	Debit	Credit	Balance
20X1				
Mar. 12	P1		900	900
Mar. 20	CD1	900		0

Accounts Payable — 200

Date	Ref.	Debit	Credit	Balance
20X1				
Mar. 31	P1		3,700	3,700
Mar. 31	CD1	1,700		2,000

Purchases Discounts — 502

Date	Ref.	Debit	Credit	Balance
20X1				
Mar. 31	CD1		18	18

Entries listed in the *Other* column are posted individually to the general ledger accounts.

Supplies — 170

Date	Ref.	Debit	Credit	Balance
20X1				
Mar. 15	CD1	250		250

Rent Expense — 540

Date	Ref.	Debit	Credit	Balance
20X1				
Mar. 1	CD1	1,200		1,200

Utilities Expense — 550

Date	Ref.	Debit	Credit	Balance
20X1				
Mar. 10	CD1	400		400

General journal entries. The general journal is used for adjusting entries, closing entries, correcting entries, and all transactions that do not belong in one of the special journals. For example, if a company uses only the special journals discussed in this chapter, purchase returns and allowances and sales returns and allowances would have to be recorded in the general journal.

If a general journal entry involves an account in a subsidiary ledger, the transaction must be posted to both the general ledger control account and the subsidiary ledger account. Both account numbers are placed in the general journal's reference column to indicate that the entry has been posted correctly.

General Journal   GJ1

Date	Account Title and Description	Ref.	Debit	Credit
20X1				
Mar. 5	Sales Returns & Allowances	401	200	
	Accounts Receivable–T. Smith	110/AR5		200
	Credit Memo #100–T. Smith			

Sales Returns & Allowances   401

Date	Explanation	Ref.	Debit	Credit	Balance
20X1					
Mar. 5	CM #100–T. Smith	GJ1	200		200

General journal entries that affect control accounts must be posted to both the general ledger and the subsidiary ledger accounts.

Accounts Receivable   110

Date	Explanation	Ref.	Debit	Credit	Balance
20X1					4,500
Mar. 5	CM #100–T. Smith	GJ1		200	4,300

T. Smith   AR5

Date	Explanation	Ref.	Debit	Credit	Balance
20X1					
Mar. 1	Credit purchase	S1	1,000		1,000
Mar. 5	CM #100–T. Smith	GJ1		200	800

Cash is a company's most liquid asset, which means it can easily be used to acquire other assets, buy services, or satisfy obligations. For financial reporting purposes, cash includes currency and coin on hand, money orders and checks made payable to the company, and available balances in checking and savings accounts. Most companies report cash and cash equivalents together. **Cash equivalents** are highly liquid, short-term investments that usually mature within three months of their purchase date. Examples of cash equivalents include U.S. treasury bills, money market funds, and commercial paper, which is short-term corporate debt.

Cash Controls

Cash is a liquid, portable, and desirable asset. Therefore, a company must have adequate controls to prevent theft or other misuses of cash. The same control activities introduced in the first chapter of this book have specific applications when cash is involved. These control activities include segregation of duties, proper authorization, adequate documents and records, physical controls, and independent checks on performance.

- **Segregation of duties.** Cash is generally received at cash registers or through the mail. The employee who receives cash should be different from the employee who records cash receipts, and a third employee should be responsible for making cash deposits at the bank. Having different employees perform these tasks helps minimize the potential for theft.

- **Proper authorization.** Only certain people should be authorized to handle cash or make cash transactions on behalf of the company. In addition, all cash expenses should be authorized by responsible managers.

- **Adequate documents and records.** Company managers and others who are responsible for safeguarding a company's cash assets must have confidence in the accuracy and legitimacy of source documents that involve cash. Important documents such as checks, are prenumbered in sequential order to help managers ascertain the disposition of each document. This helps prevent transactions from being recorded twice or from not being recorded at all. In addition, documents should be forwarded to the accounting department soon after their creation so that recordkeeping can be handled professionally and efficiently. Allowing documents that describe cash transactions to go unrecorded for an unnecessarily long period of time increases the likelihood that fraudulent or inaccurate records will pass undetected through the accounting department.

- **Physical controls.** Cash on hand must be physically secure. This is accomplished in a variety of ways. Cash registers should contain only enough cash to handle customer transactions. When a cashier finishes a shift—or perhaps more frequently— excess cash should be moved from cash registers to a safe or another location that provides additional security. In addition, daily bank deposits are made so that excess cash does not remain on the premises. Blank checks, which can be used for forgery, are stored in locked, fireproof files.

- **Independent checks on performance.** Employees who handle cash or who record cash transactions must be prepared for independent checks on their performance. These checks should be done periodically and may be done without forewarning. Having a supervisor verify the accuracy of a cashier's drawer on a daily basis is an example of this type of control.

- **Other cash controls.** Most companies bond individuals that handle cash. A company **bonds** an employee by paying a bonding company for insurance against theft by the employee. If the employee then steals, the bonding company reimburses the company. Companies may also rotate employees from one task to another. Embezzlement or serious mistakes may be uncovered when a new employee takes over a task. Although specific cash controls vary from one company to the next, all companies must implement effective cash controls.

The Petty Cash Fund

Companies normally use checks to pay their obligations because checks provide a record of each payment. Companies also maintain a **petty cash fund** to pay for small, miscellaneous expenditures such as stamps, small delivery charges, or emergency supplies. The size of a petty cash fund varies depending on the needs of the business. A petty cash fund should be small enough so that it does not unnecessarily tie up company assets or become a target for theft, but it should be large enough to lessen the inconvenience associated with frequently replenishing the fund. For this reason, companies typically establish a petty cash fund that needs to be replenished every two to four weeks.

Companies assign responsibility for the petty cash fund to a person called the petty cash custodian or petty cashier. To establish a petty cash fund, someone must write a check to the petty cash custodian, who cashes the check and keeps the money in a locked file or cash box. The journal entry to record the creation of a petty cash fund appears below.

	General Journal				GJ1
Date	Account Title and Description	Ref.	Debit	Credit
20X8				
Apr. 1	Petty Cash		150	
	Cash			150
	Establish petty cash fund			

Most companies would record this entry—or any other entry that credits cash—in the cash disbursements special journal, but the illustrations in this chapter use the general journal to eliminate journal columns that are not relevant to this discussion and to conform with this subject's presentation in most textbooks.

Whenever someone in the company requests petty cash, the petty cash custodian prepares a voucher that identifies the date, amount, recipient, and reason for the cash disbursement. For control purposes, vouchers are sequentially prenumbered and signed by both the person requesting the cash and the custodian. After the cash is spent, receipts or other relevant documents should be returned to the petty cash custodian, who attaches them to the voucher. All vouchers are kept with the petty cash fund until the fund is replenished, so the total amount of the vouchers and the remaining cash in the fund should always equal the amount assigned to the fund.

When the fund requires more cash or at the end of an accounting period, the petty cash custodian requests a check for the difference between the cash on hand and the total assigned to the fund. At this time, the person who provides cash to the custodian should examine the vouchers to verify their legitimacy. The transaction that replenishes the petty cash fund is recorded with a compound entry that debits all relevant asset or expense accounts and credits cash. Consider the journal entry below, which is made after the custodian requests $130 to replenish the petty cash fund and submits vouchers that fall into one of three categories.

General Journal				GJ12
Date	Account Title and Description	Ref.	Debit	Credit
20X8				
Apr. 30	Office Supplies		55	
	Postage Expense		40	
	Transportation Expense		35	
	Cash			130
	Replenish petty cash fund			

Notice that the petty cash account is debited or credited only when the fund is established or when the size of the fund is increased or decreased, not when the fund is replenished.

If the voucher amounts do not equal the cash needed to replenish the fund, the difference is recorded in an account named *cash over and short*. This account is debited when there is a cash shortage and credited when there is a cash overage. Cash over and short appears on the income statement as a miscellaneous expense if the account has a debit balance or as a miscellaneous revenue if the account has a credit balance. In the journal entry below, the vouchers total $130 but the fund needs $135, so the entry includes a $5 debit to the cash over and short account.

General Journal   GJ12

Date	Account Title and Description	Ref.	Debit	Credit
20X8				
Apr. 30	Office Supplies		55	
	Postage Expense		40	
	Transportation Expense		35	
	Cash Over and Short		5	
	Cash			135
	Replenish petty cash fund			

If the vouchers total $130 but the fund needs only $125, the journal entry includes a $5 credit to the cash over and short account.

General Journal   GJ12

Date	Account Title and Description	Ref.	Debit	Credit
20X8				
Apr. 30	Office Supplies		55	
	Postage Expense		40	
	Transportation Expense		35	
	Cash			125
	Cash Over and Short			5
	Replenish petty cash fund			

Bank Reconciliation

Banks usually send customers a monthly statement that shows the account's beginning balance (the previous statement's ending balance), all transactions that affect the account's balance during the month, and the account's ending balance.

First National Bank
1234 First Avenue
Primo Vista, CA 90783-1409

Statement of Account
109-654-5454-45

April 30, 20X8

Vector Management Group
3214 Tangent Ln.
Circle Park, CA 90778-3421

Balance Last Statement	7,358
Total Credits	14,083
Total Debits	13,239
Balance This Statement	8,202

Date	Check	Debits		Credits		Balance
4/1/20X8						7,358
4/2/20X8				3,200		10,558
4/2/20X8	1541	152				10,406
4/4/20X8	1547	330				10,076
4/5/20X8	1551	18				10,058
4/6/20X8		20	SC			10,038
4/6/20X8	1553	152				9,886
4/7/20X8	1554	87				9,799
4/9/20X8				2,800		12,599
4/10/20X8	1555	1,524				11,075
4/11/20X8	1556	765				10,310
4/12/20X8		253	DM			10,057
4/12/20X8	1557	32				10,025
4/13/20X8	1558	304				9,721
4/14/20X8	1559	3,227				6,494
4/16/20X8				3,100		9,594
4/17/20X8	1560	81				9,513
4/19/20X8		50	SC			9,463
4/19/20X8	1561	152				9,311
4/20/20X8	1562	66				9,245
4/20/20X8	1563	1,325				7,920
4/21/20X8	1566	358				7,562
4/23/20X8				3,400		10,962
4/24/20X8	1567	429				10,533
4/24/20X8		345	NSF			10,188
4/25/20X8				1,565	CM	11,753
4/27/20X8	1568	3,188				8,565
4/30/20X8	1569	381				8,184
4/30/20X8				18	INT	8,202

Symbol key: CM = Credit Memo (see attachment)   INT = Interest
             DD = Direct Deposit   NSF = Not Sufficient Funds
             DM = Debit Memo (see attachment)   SC = Service Charge

The ending balance on a bank statement almost never agrees with the balance in a company's corresponding general ledger account. After receiving the bank statement, therefore, the company prepares a **bank reconciliation,** which identifies each difference between the company's records and the bank's records. The normal differences identified in a bank reconciliation will be discussed separately. These differences are referred to as reconciling items. A bank reconciliation begins by showing the bank statement's ending balance and the company's balance (book balance) in the cash account on the same date.

Vector Management Group
Bank Reconciliation
April 30, 20X8

Bank statement balance $ 8,202	Book balance	$ 6,370

Deposits in transit. Most companies make frequent cash deposits. Therefore, company records may show one or more deposits, usually made on the last day included on the bank statement, that do not appear on the bank statement. These deposits are called deposits in transit and cause the bank statement balance to understate the company's actual cash balance. Since deposits in transit have already been recorded in the company's books as cash receipts, they must be added to the bank statement balance. The Vector Management Group made a $3,000 deposit on the afternoon of April 30 that does not appear on the statement, so this deposit in transit is added to the bank statement balance.

Vector Management Group
Bank Reconciliation
April 30, 20X8

Bank statement balance $ 8,202	Book balance	$ 6,370
Add: Deposits in transit 3,000		
11,202		

Outstanding checks. A check that a company mails to a creditor may take several days to pass through the mail, be processed and deposited by the creditor, and then clear the banking system. Therefore, company records may include a number of checks that do not appear on the bank statement. These checks are called outstanding checks and cause the bank statement balance to overstate the company's actual cash balance. Since outstanding checks have already been recorded in the company's books as cash disbursements, they must be subtracted from the bank statement balance.

Vector Management Group
Bank Reconciliation
April 30, 20X8

Bank statement balance	$ 8,202	Book balance	$ 6,370
Add: Deposits in transit	3,000		
	11,202		

Less: Outstanding checks

1552	$1,057		
1564	245		
1565	108		
1570	359		
1571	802		
1572	1,409	(3,980)	

Adjusted bank balance $ 7,222

Automatic withdrawals and deposits. Companies may authorize a bank to automatically transfer funds into or out of their account. Automatic withdrawals from the account are used to pay for loans (notes or mortgages payable), monthly utility bills, or other liabilities. Automatic deposits occur when the company's checking account receives automatic fund transfers from customers or other sources or when the bank collects notes receivable payments on behalf of the company.

Banks use **debit memoranda** to notify companies about automatic withdrawals, and they use **credit memoranda** to notify companies about automatic deposits. The names applied to these memoranda may seem confusing at first glance because the company credits (decreases) its cash account upon receiving debit memoranda from the bank, and the company debits (increases) its cash account upon receiving credit memoranda from the bank. To the bank, however, a company's checking account balance is a liability rather than an asset. Therefore, from the bank's perspective, the terms *debit* and *credit* are correctly applied to the memoranda. If this still seems confusing, you may want to review the chart on page 19 and think about how the company classifies their account as an asset while the bank classifies the company's account as a liability.

A credit memorandum attached to the Vector Management Group's bank statement describes the bank's collection of a $1,500 note receivable along with $90 in interest. The bank deducted $25 for this service, so the automatic deposit was for $1,565. The bank statement also includes a debit memorandum describing a $253 automatic withdrawal for a utility payment. Unlike deposits in transit or outstanding checks, which are already recorded in the company's books, automatic withdrawals and deposits are often brought to the company's attention for the first time when the bank statement is received. On the bank reconciliation, add unrecorded automatic deposits to the company's book balance, and subtract unrecorded automatic withdrawals.

Vector Management Group
Bank Reconciliation
April 30, 20X8

Bank statement balance	$ 8,202	Book balance		$ 6,370
Add: Deposits in transit	3,000	Add: Note collection		
	11,202	plus interest		
		less bank fee	$1,565	
Less: Outstanding checks		Less: Utility payment	$253	
1552 $1,057				
1564 245				
1565 108				
1570 359				
1571 802				
1572 1,409	(3,980)			
Adjusted bank balance	$ 7,222			

Because reconciling items that affect the book balance on a bank reconciliation have not been recorded in the company's books, they must be journalized and posted to the general ledger accounts. The $1,565 credit memorandum requires a compound journal entry involving four accounts. Cash is debited for $1,565, bank fees expense is debited for $25, notes receivable is credited for $1,500, and interest revenue is credited for $90.

		General Journal			GJ14
Date	Account Title and Description	Ref.	Debit	Credit
20X8				
Apr. 30	Cash		1,565	
	Bank Fees Expense		25	
	Notes Receivable			1,500
	Interest Revenue			90
	Bank collection of note			

If the Vector Management Group had previously made adjusting entries to accrue all of the interest revenue (by debiting interest receivable and crediting interest revenue), then interest receivable rather than interest revenue would need to be credited for $90 in the journal entry shown above.

The automatic withdrawal requires a simple journal entry that debits utilities expense and credits cash for $253.

		General Journal			GJ14
Date	Account Title and Description	Ref.	Debit	Credit
20X8				
Apr. 30	Utilities Expense		253	
	Cash			253
	Utility payment made by bank			

Interest earned. Banks often pay interest on checking account balances. Interest income reported on the bank statement has usually not been accrued by the company and, therefore, must be added to the company's book balance on the bank reconciliation. The final transaction listed on the Vector Management Group's bank statement on page 120 is for $18 in interest that has not been accrued, so this amount is added to the right side of the bank reconciliation shown below.

Vector Management Group
Bank Reconciliation
April 30, 20X8

Bank statement balance	$ 8,202	Book balance			$ 6,370
Add: Deposits in transit	3,000	Add: Note collection			
	11,202	plus interest			
		less bank fee	$1,565		
		Interest earned	18	1,583	
					7,953
Less: Outstanding checks		Less: Utility payment	$253		
1552	$1,057				
1564	245				
1565	108				
1570	359				
1571	802				
1572	1,409	(3,980)			
Adjusted bank balance	$ 7,222				

The interest revenue must be journalized and posted to the general ledger cash account. In the journal entry below, cash is debited for $18 and interest revenue is credited for $18.

General Journal   GJ14

Date	Account Title and Description	Ref.	Debit	Credit
20X8				
Apr. 30	Cash		18	
	Interest Revenue			18
	Checking account interest			

Bank service charges. Banks often require customers to pay monthly account fees, check printing fees, safe-deposit box rental fees, and other fees. Unrecorded service charges must be subtracted from the company's book balance on the bank reconciliation. The Vector Management Group's bank statement on page 120 includes a $20 service charge for check printing and a $50 service charge for the rental of a safe-deposit box.

Vector Management Group
Bank Reconciliation
April 30, 20X8

Bank statement balance	$ 8,202	Book balance				$ 6,370
Add: Deposits in transit	3,000	Add: Note collection				
	11,202	plus interest				
		less bank fee	$1,565			
		Interest earned	18	1,583		
				7,953		

Less: Outstanding checks			Less: Utility payment	$253	
1552	$1,057		Check printing	20	
1564	245		Safe-deposit box		
1565	108		rental	50	
1570	359				
1571	802				
1572	1,409	(3,980)			

Adjusted bank balance $ 7,222

Although separate journal entries for each expense can be made, it is simpler to combine them, so bank fees expense is debited for $70 and cash is credited for $70.

General Journal   GJ14

Date	Account Title and Description	Ref.	Debit	Credit
20X8				
Apr. 30	Bank Fees Expense		70	
	Cash			70
	Check printing/deposit box			

NSF (not sufficient funds) checks. A check previously recorded as part of a deposit may bounce because there are not sufficient funds in the issuer's checking account. When this happens, the bank returns the check to the depositor and deducts the check amount from the depositor's account. Therefore, NSF checks must be subtracted from the company's book balance on the bank reconciliation. The Vector Management Group's bank statement includes an NSF check for $345 from Hosta, Inc.

Vector Management Group
Bank Reconciliation
April 30, 20X8

Bank statement balance	$ 8,202	Book balance		$ 6,370
Add: Deposits in transit	3,000	Add: Note collection		
	11,202	plus interest		
		less bank fee	$1,565	
		Interest earned	18	1,583
				7,953
Less: Outstanding checks		Less: Utility payment	$253	
1552	$1,057	Check printing	20	
1564	245	Safe deposit box		
1565	108	rental	50	
1570	359	NSF Hosta, Inc.	345	
1571	802			
1572	1,409	(3,980)		
Adjusted bank balance	$ 7,222			

Since the NSF check has previously been recorded as a cash receipt, a journal entry is necessary to update the company's books. Therefore, a $345 debit is made to increase the accounts receivable balance of Hosta, Inc., and a $345 credit is made to decrease cash.

General Journal   **GJ14**

Date	Account Title and Description	Ref.	Debit	Credit
20X8				
Apr. 30	Accounts Receivable–Hosta, Inc.		345	
	Cash			345
	NSF from Hosta, Inc.			

Errors. Companies and banks sometimes make errors. Therefore, each transaction on the bank statement should be double-checked. If the bank incorrectly recorded a transaction, the bank must be contacted, and the bank balance must be adjusted on the bank reconciliation. If the company incorrectly recorded a transaction, the book balance must be adjusted on the bank reconciliation and a correcting entry must be journalized and posted to the general ledger. While reviewing the bank statement, Vector Management Group discovers that check #1569 for $381, which was made payable to an advertising agency named Ad It Up, had been incorrectly entered in the cash disbursements journal for $318. This error is a reconciling item because the company's general ledger cash account is overstated by $63.

Vector Management Group
Bank Reconciliation
April 30, 20X8

Bank statement balance	$ 8,202	Book balance				$ 6,370
Add: Deposits in transit	3,000	Add: Note collection				
	11,202	plus interest				
		less bank fee		$1,565		
		Interest earned		18	1,583	
						7,953
Less: Outstanding checks		Less: Utility payment		$253		
1552	$1,057	Check printing		20		
1564	245	Safe deposit box				
1565	108	rental		50		
1570	359	NSF Hosta, Inc.		345		
1571	802	Error check #1569		63	(731)	
1572	1,409	(3,980)				
Adjusted bank balance	$ 7,222	Adjusted book balance				$ 7,222

When all differences between the ending bank statement balance and book balance have been identified and entered on the bank reconciliation, the adjusted bank balance and adjusted book balance are identical.

Since the Vector Management Group paid Ad It Up $63 more than the books show, a $63 debit is made to decrease the accounts payable balance owed to Ad It Up, and a $63 credit is made to decrease cash.

	General Journal				GJ14
Date	Account Title and Description	Ref.	Debit	Credit
20X8				
Apr. 30	Accounts Payable–Ad It Up		63	
	Cash			63
	Correction check #1569			

Credit Card Sales

Retail companies, which sell merchandise in small quantities directly to consumers, often receive a significant portion of their revenue through credit card sales. Some credit card receipts, specifically those involving credit cards issued by banks, are deposited along with cash and checks made payable to the company. The company receives cash for these credit card sales immediately. Because banks that issue credit cards to customers handle billing, collections, and related expenses, they usually charge companies between 2% and 5% of the sales price. This fee is deducted when the receipts are deposited in the company's bank account, so these credit card receipts are slightly more complicated to record than other types of cash deposits. If a company deposits credit card receipts totaling $1,000 and the fee is 3%, the company makes a compound entry that debits cash for $970, debits credit card expense for $30 (3% of $1,000), and credits sales for $1,000.

	General Journal				GJ64
Date	Account Title and Description	Ref.	Debit	Credit
20X5				
Dec. 17	Cash		970	
	Credit Card Expense		30	
	Sales			1,000
	Deposit credit card receipts			

Some credit card receipts must be treated as receivables rather than cash. For example, many gas stations and department stores provide customers with credit cards that can be used to buy goods or services only at the issuer's place of business. When a customer makes a purchase, the company must debit the customer's account and credit the sales account. There are also some major credit cards that are not issued by banks, and receipts from these cards must be sent to the credit card company for reimbursement rather than deposited at a bank. After submitting credit card receipts totaling $1,000 directly to a credit card company, the company that makes the sale records the entry by debiting accounts receivable and crediting sales.

	General Journal				GJ64
Date	Account Title and Description	Ref.	Debit	Credit
20X5				
Dec. 17	Accounts Receivable–Card Issuer		1,000	
	Sales			1,000
	Credit card sales			

The credit card company deducts their fee before paying the company that made the sale. Upon receiving payment, the company that made the sale debits cash, debits credit card expense, and credits accounts receivable.

	General Journal				GJ64
Date	Account Title and Description	Ref.	Debit	Credit
20X5				
Dec. 29	Cash		970	
	Credit Card Expense		30	
	Accounts Receivable–Card Issuer			1,000
	Payment from card issuer			

Recording credit card expenses after receiving payment, as in the example above, is convenient because a compound journal entry is all that is needed. However, if the sale occurs during one accounting period and the payment is not received until the next accounting period, an adjusting entry must be made, if the amount of credit card expense is significant, to prevent the matching principle from being violated. The matching principle requires that expenses be recognized during the same accounting period as the revenues they help to generate. If the payment in the previous example had not yet been received at the close of an accounting period, the company would make an adjusting entry that debits credit card expense for $30 and credits accounts receivable for $30.

General Journal　　　　　　　　　　　　　GJ64

Date	Account Title and Description	Ref.	Debit	Credit
20X5				
Dec. 31	Credit Card Expense		30	
	Accounts Receivable–Card Issuer			30
	Accrue credit expense			

Then, after the payment arrives, cash is debited for $970 and accounts receivable is credited for $970.

General Journal　　　　　　　　　　　　　GJ65

Date	Account Title and Description	Ref.	Debit	Credit
20X6				
Jan. 5	Cash		970	
	Accounts Receivable–Card Issuer			970
	Payment from card issuer			

Accounts receivable are amounts that customers owe the company for normal credit purchases. Since accounts receivable are generally collected within two months of the sale, they are considered a current asset and usually appear on balance sheets below short-term investments and above inventory.

Notes receivable are amounts owed to the company by customers or others who have signed formal promissory notes in acknowledgment of their debts. Promissory notes strengthen a company's legal claim against those who fail to pay as promised. The maturity date of a note determines whether it is placed with current assets or long-term assets on the balance sheet. Notes that are due in one year or less are considered current assets, and notes that are due in more than one year are considered long-term assets.

Accounts receivable and notes receivable that result from company sales are called **trade receivables,** but there are other types of receivables as well. For example, interest revenue from notes or other interest-bearing assets is accrued at the end of each accounting period and placed in an account named *interest receivable.* Wage advances, formal loans to employees, or loans to other companies create other types of receivables. If significant, these nontrade receivables are usually listed in separate categories on the balance sheet because each type of nontrade receivable has distinct risk factors and liquidity characteristics.

Receivables of all types are normally reported on the balance sheet at their **net realizable value,** which is the amount the company expects to receive in cash.

Evaluating Accounts Receivable

Business owners know that some customers who receive credit will never pay their account balances. These uncollectible accounts are also called bad debts. Companies use two methods to account for bad debts: the direct write-off method and the allowance method.

Direct write-off method. For tax purposes, companies must use the direct write-off method, under which bad debts are recognized only after the company is certain the debt will not be paid. Before determining that an account balance is uncollectible, a company generally makes several attempts to collect the debt from the customer. Recognizing the bad debt requires a journal entry that increases a bad debts expense account and decreases accounts receivable. If a customer named J. Smith fails to pay a $225 balance, for example, the company records the write-off by debiting bad debts expense and crediting accounts receivable from J. Smith.

General Journal				GJ48
Date	Account Title and Description	Ref.	Debit	Credit
20X6				
May 31	Bad Debts Expense		225	
	Accounts Receivable–J. Smith			225
	Write off J. Smith's account			

The Internal Revenue Service permits companies to take a tax deduction for bad debts only after specific uncollectible accounts have been identified. Unless a company's uncollectible accounts represent an insignificant percentage of their sales, however, they may not use the direct write-off method for financial reporting purposes. Since several months may pass between the time that a sale occurs and the time that a company realizes that a customer's account is uncollectible, the matching principle, which requires that revenues and related expenses be matched in the same accounting period, would often be violated if the direct write-off method were used. Therefore, most companies use the direct write-off method on their tax returns but use the allowance method on financial statements.

Allowance method. Under the allowance method, an adjustment is made at the end of each accounting period to estimate bad debts based on the business activity from that accounting period. Established companies rely on past experience to estimate unrealized bad debts, but new companies must rely on published industry averages until they have sufficient experience to make their own estimates.

The adjusting entry to estimate the expected value of bad debts does not reduce accounts receivable directly. Accounts receivable is a control account that must have the same balance as the combined balance of every individual account in the accounts receivable subsidiary ledger. Since the specific customer accounts that will become uncollectible are not yet known when the adjusting entry is made, a contra-asset account named *allowance for bad debts,* which is sometimes called *allowance for doubtful accounts,* is subtracted from accounts receivable to show the net realizable value of accounts receivable on the balance sheet.

If at the end of its first accounting period a company estimates that $5,000 in accounts receivable will become uncollectible, the necessary adjusting entry debits bad debts expense for $5,000 and credits allowance for bad debts for $5,000.

	General Journal			GJ32
Date	Account Title and Description	Ref.	Debit	Credit
20X5				
Dec. 31	Bad Debts Expense		5,000	
	Allowance for Bad Debts			5,000
	Estimate of bad debts			

After the entry shown above is made, the accounts receivable subsidiary ledger still shows the full amount each customer owes, the balance of the control account (accounts receivable) agrees with the total balance in the subsidiary ledger, the credit balance in the contra asset account (allowance for bad debts) can be subtracted from the debit balance in accounts receivable to show the net realizable value of accounts receivable, and a reasonable estimate of bad debts expense is recognized in the appropriate accounting period.

When a specific customer's account is identified as uncollectible, it is written off against the balance in the allowance for bad debts account. For example, J. Smith's uncollectible balance of $225 is removed from the books by debiting allowance for bad debts and crediting accounts receivable. Remember, general journal entries that affect a control account must be posted to both the control account and the specific account in the subsidiary ledger.

General Journal   GJ48

Date	Account Title and Description	Ref.	Debit	Credit
20X6				
May 31	Allowance for Bad Debts	115	225	
	Accounts Receivable–J. Smith	110/AR91		225
	Write off J. Smith's account			

General Ledger Accounts

Allowance for Bad Debts 115

Date	Ref.	Debit	Credit	Balance
20X6				5,000
May 31	GJ48	225		4,775

Accounts Receivable 110

Date	Ref.	Debit	Credit	Balance
20X6				100,000
May 31	GJ48		225	99,775

Accounts Receivable
Subsidiary Ledger

J. Smith   AR91

Date	Ref.	Debit	Credit	Balance
20X6				225
May 31	GJ48		225	0

Under the allowance method, a write-off does not change the net realizable value of accounts receivable. It simply reduces accounts receivable and allowance for bad debts by equivalent amounts.

	Before writing off J. Smith's account	After writing off J. Smith's account
Accounts Receivable	$100,000	$99,775
Less: Allowance for Bad Debts	(5,000)	(4,775)
Net Realizable Value	$ 95,000	$95,000

Customers whose accounts have already been written off as uncollectible will sometimes pay their debts. When this happens, two entries are needed to correct the company's accounting records and show that the customer paid the outstanding balance. The first entry reinstates the customer's accounts receivable balance by debiting accounts receivable and crediting allowance for bad debts. As in the previous example, the debit to accounts receivable must be posted to the general ledger control account and to the appropriate subsidiary ledger account.

General Journal   GJ56

Date	Account Title and Description	Ref.	Debit	Credit
20X6				
Aug. 11	Accounts Receivable–J. Smith	110/AR91	225	
	Allowance for Bad Debts	115		225
	Reverse J. Smith write-off			

General Ledger Accounts

Accounts Receivable Subsidiary Ledger

Accounts Receivable   110

Date	Ref.	Debit	Credit	Balance
20X6				100,000
May 31	GJ48		225	99,775
Aug. 11	GJ56	225		100,000

J. Smith   AR91

Date	Ref.	Debit	Credit	Balance
20X6				225
May 31	GJ48		225	0
Aug. 11	GJ56	225		225

Allowance for Bad Debts   115

Date	Ref.	Debit	Credit	Balance
20X6				5,000
May 31	GJ48	225		4,775
Aug. 11	GJ56		225	5,000

The second entry records the customer's payment by debiting cash and crediting accounts receivable. Most companies record cash receipts in a cash receipts journal. Since a special journal's column totals are posted to the general ledger at the end of each accounting period, the posting to J. Smith's account is the only one shown with the cash receipts journal entry in the illustration below. Page 110 describes the cash receipts journal in detail.

		Cash Receipts Journal					CR81
Date	Account	Ref.	Cash (Dr.)	Sales Discounts (Dr.)	Accounts Receivable (Cr.)	Sales (Cr.)	Other (Cr.)
20X6							
Aug. 11	AR–J. Smith	AR91	225		225		

		J. Smith				AR91
Date	Explanation	Ref.	Debit	Credit	Balance
20X6					225
May 31	Write off account	GJ48		225	0
Aug. 11	Reverse write-off	GJ56	225		225
11	Payment	CR81		225	0

In the future when management looks at J. Smith's payment history, the account's activity will show the eventual collection of the amount owed.

Textbooks usually explain the repayment of previously written-off debts using the general journal. If you use the general journal for the entry shown in the cash receipts journal on the previous page, you post the entry directly to cash and accounts receivable in the general ledger and also to J. Smith's account in the accounts receivable subsidiary ledger.

General Journal   GJ56

Date	Account Title and Description	Ref.	Debit	Credit
20X6				
Aug. 11	Accounts Receivable–J. Smith	110/AR91	225	
	Allowance for Bad Debts	115		225
	Reverse J. Smith write-off			
11	Cash	100	225	
	Accounts Receivable–J. Smith	110/AR91		225
	Received payment from J. Smith			

General Ledger Accounts

Cash   100

Date	Ref.	Debit	Credit	Balance
20X6				6,075
Aug. 11	GJ56	225		6,300

Accounts Receivable   110

Date	Ref.	Debit	Credit	Balance
20X6				100,000
May 31	GJ48		225	99,775
Aug. 11	GJ56	225		100,000
11	GJ56		225	99,775

Accounts Receivable Subsidiary Ledger

J. Smith   AR91

Date	Ref.	Debit	Credit	Balance
20X6				225
May 31	GJ48		225	0
Aug. 11	GJ56	225		225
11	GJ56		225	0

Estimating Bad Debts Under the Allowance Method

Percentage of total accounts receivable method. One way companies derive an estimate for the value of bad debts under the allowance method is to calculate bad debts as a percentage of the accounts receivable balance. If a company has $100,000 in accounts receivable at the end of an accounting period and company records indicate that, on average, 5% of total accounts receivable become uncollectible, the allowance for bad debts account must be adjusted to have a credit balance of $5,000 (5% of $100,000).

Unless actual write-offs during the just-completed accounting period perfectly matched the balance assigned to the allowance for bad debts account at the close of the previous accounting period, the account will have an existing balance. If write-offs were less than expected, the account will have a credit balance, and if write-offs were greater than expected, the account will have a debit balance. Assuming that the allowance for bad debts account has a $200 debit balance when the adjusting entry is made, a $5,200 adjusting entry is necessary to give the account a credit balance of $5,000.

General Journal — GJ64

Date	Account Title and Description	Ref.	Debit	Credit
20X6				
Dec. 31	Bad Debts Expense	570	5,200	
	Allowance for Bad Debts	115		5,200
	Estimate of bad debts			

Bad Debts Expense — 570

Date	Explanation	Ref.	Debit	Credit	Balance
20X6					
Dec. 31	Estimate of bad debts	GJ64	5,200		5,200

Allowance for Bad Debts — 115

Date	Explanation	Ref.	Debit	Credit	Balance
20X6					(200)
Dec. 31	Estimate of bad debts	GJ64		5,200	5,000

If the allowance for bad debts account had a $300 credit balance instead of a $200 debit balance, a $4,700 adjusting entry would be needed to give the account a credit balance of $5,000.

Aging method. In general, the longer an account balance is overdue, the less likely the debt is to be paid. Therefore, many companies maintain an **accounts receivable aging schedule,** which categorizes each customer's credit purchases by the length of time they have been outstanding. Each category's overall balance is multiplied by an estimated percentage of uncollectibility for that category, and the total of all such calculations serves as the estimate of bad debts. The accounts receivable aging schedule shown below includes five categories for classifying the age of unpaid credit purchases.

Accounts Receivable Aging Schedule
December 31, 20X6

| Customer | Balance | Current | Days Past Due | | | |
			1 to 30	31 to 60	61 to 90	Over 90
C. Aaron	$ 2,000	$ 2,000				
B. Ambroz	1,900	1,100	$ 800			
J. Baker	1,300			$1,100	$ 200	
W. Bruce	1,500	800	700			
H. Bunica	2,000	2,000				
K. Carter	600					$ 600
E. Cline	2,700	2,700				
All Others	88,000	71,400	12,500	1,900	800	1,400
Totals	$100,000	$80,000	$14,000	$3,000	$1,000	$2,000
Percentage		1%	10%	30%	50%	70%
Estimated Bad Debts	$ 5,000	$ 800	$ 1,400	$ 900	$ 500	$1,400

In this example, estimated bad debts are $5,000. If the account has an existing credit balance of $400, the adjusting entry includes a $4,600 debit to bad debts expense and a $4,600 credit to allowance for bad debts.

General Journal   GJ64

Date	Account Title and Description	Ref.	Debit	Credit
20X6				
Dec. 31	Bad Debts Expense		4,600	
	Allowance for Bad Debts			4,600
	Estimate of bad debts			

Percentage of credit sales method. Some companies estimate bad debts as a percentage of credit sales. If a company has $500,000 in credit sales during an accounting period and company records indicate that, on average, 1% of credit sales become uncollectible, the adjusting entry at the end of the accounting period debits bad debts expense for $5,000 and credits allowance for bad debts for $5,000.

General Journal					GJ64
Date	Account Title and Description	Ref.	Debit	Credit
20X6				
Dec. 31	Bad Debts Expense		5,000	
	Allowance for Bad Debts			5,000
	Estimate of bad debts			

Companies that use the percentage of credit sales method base the adjusting entry solely on total credit sales and ignore any existing balance in the allowance for bad debts account. If estimates fail to match actual bad debts, the percentage rate used to estimate bad debts is adjusted on future estimates.

Factoring Receivables

Companies sometimes need cash before customers pay their account balances. In such situations, the company may choose to sell accounts receivable to another company that specializes in collections. This process is called factoring, and the company that purchases accounts receivable is often called a factor. The factor usually charges between one and fifteen percent of the account balances. The reason for such a wide range in fees is that the receivables may be factored with or without recourse. **Recourse** means the company factoring the receivables agrees to reimburse the factor for uncollectible accounts. Low percentage rates are usually offered only when recourse is provided.

Suppose a company factors $500,000 in accounts receivable at a rate of 3%. The company records this sale of accounts receivable by debiting cash for $485,000, debiting factoring expense (or service charge expense) for $15,000, and crediting accounts receivable for $500,000.

	General Journal			GJ44
Date	Account Title and Description	Ref.	Debit	Credit
20X1				
May 14	Cash		485,000	
	Factoring Expense		15,000	
	Accounts Receivable			500,000
	Factor accounts worth $500,000			

In practice, the credit to accounts receivable would need to identify the specific subsidiary ledger accounts that were factored, although to simplify the example this is not done here.

Notes Receivable

Companies classify the promissory notes they hold as notes receivable. A simple promissory note appears below.

$1,000
(Principal Amount)

Surf City, California   June 18, 20X1
(Location and Date)

4 months after date   Jim Radd   promises to pay
(Name of Maker)

to the order of   Surf Breaker West
(Name of Payee)

for value received with annual interest at   9 %
(Interest Rate)

Jim Radd
(Signature of Maker)

The face value of a note is called the **principal,** which equals the initial amount of credit provided. The **maker** of a note is the party who receives the credit and promises to pay the note's holder. The maker classifies the note as a note payable. The **payee** is the party that holds the note and receives payment from the maker when the note is due. The payee classifies the note as a note receivable.

Calculating interest. Notes generally specify an interest rate, which is used to determine how much interest the maker of the note must pay in addition to the principal. Interest on short-term notes is calculated according to the following formula:

$$\text{Principal} \times \frac{\text{Annual}}{\text{Interest Rate}} \times \frac{\text{Time Period}}{\text{in Years}} = \text{Interest}$$

For example, interest on a four-month, 9%, $1,000 note equals $30.

$$\$1,000 \times .09 \times \frac{4}{12} = \$30$$

When a note's due date is expressed in days, the specified number of days is divided by 360 or 365 in the interest calculation. You may see either of these figures because accountants used a 360-day year to simplify their calculations before computers and calculators became widely available, and many textbooks still follow this convention. In current practice, however, financial institutions and other companies generally use a 365-day year to calculate interest. Therefore, you should be prepared to calculate interest either way.

The interest on a 90-day, 12%, $10,000 note equals $300 if a 360-day year is used to calculate interest, and the interest equals $295.89 if a 365-day year is used.

$$\$10,000 \times .12 \times \frac{90}{360} = \$300$$

$$\$10,000 \times .12 \times \frac{90}{365} = \$295.89$$

Even when a note's due date is not expressed in days, adjusting entries that recognize accrued interest are often calculated in terms of days. Suppose a company holds a four-month, 10%, $10,000 note dated October 19, 20X2. If the company uses an annual accounting period that ends on December 31, an adjusting entry that recognizes 73 days of accrued interest revenue must be made on December 31, 20X2. To determine the number of days in this situation, subtract the date of issue from the number of days in October and then add the result to the number of days in November and December ($31 - 19 = 12$; $12 + 30 + 31 = 73$). Notice that when you count days, you omit the note's issue date but include the note's due date or, in this situation, the date that the adjusting entry is made. Assuming the interest calculation uses a 365-day year, the accrued interest revenue equals $200.

$$\$10,000 \times .10 \times \frac{73}{365} = \$200$$

The adjusting entry debits interest receivable and credits interest revenue.

General Journal				GJ85
Date	Account Title and Description	Ref.	Debit	Credit
20X2				
Dec. 31	Interest Receivable		200	
	Interest Revenue			200
	Accrue interest on note			

Interest on long-term notes is calculated using the same formula that is used with short-term notes, but unpaid interest is usually added to the principal to determine interest in subsequent years. For example, a two-year, 10%, $10,000 note accrues $1,000 in interest during the first year. The principal and first year's interest equal $11,000 when compounded, so $1,100 in interest accrues during the second year.

$$\$10,000 \times .10 \times 1 = \$1,000 \quad \text{(First Year's Interest)}$$
$$\$11,000 \times .10 \times 1 = \$1,100 \quad \text{(Second Year's Interest)}$$

Recording Notes Receivable Transactions

Customers frequently sign promissory notes to settle overdue accounts receivable balances. For example, if a customer named D. Brown signs a six-month, 10%, $2,500 promissory note after falling 90 days past due on her account, the business records the event by debiting notes receivable for $2,500 and crediting accounts receivable from D. Brown for $2,500. Notice that the entry does not include interest revenue, which is not recorded until it is earned.

	General Journal			GJ33
Date	Account Title and Description	Ref.	Debit	Credit
20X8				
Apr. 26	Notes Receivable		2,500	
	Accounts Receivable–D. Brown			2,500
	Note for D. Brown's balance			

If a customer signs a promissory note in exchange for merchandise, the entry is recorded by debiting notes receivable and crediting sales.

	General Journal			GJ33
Date	Account Title and Description	Ref.	Debit	Credit
20X8				
Apr. 26	Notes Receivable		2,500	
	Sales			2,500
	Goods purchased with note			

A company that frequently exchanges goods or services for notes would probably include a debit column for notes receivable in the sales journal so that such transactions would not need to be recorded in the general journal. A separate subsidiary ledger for notes receivable may also be created. If the amount of notes receivable is significant, a company should establish a separate allowance for bad debts account for notes receivable.

When a note's maker pays according to the terms specified on the note, the note is said to be honored. Assuming that no adjusting entries have been made to accrue interest revenue, the honored note is recorded by debiting cash for the amount the customer pays, crediting notes receivable for the principal value of the note, and crediting interest revenue for the interest earned. The total interest on a six-month, 10%, $2,500 note is $125, so if D. Brown honors her note, the entry includes a $2,625 debit to cash, a $2,500 credit to notes receivable, and a $125 credit to interest revenue.

	General Journal			GJ42
Date	Account Title and Description	Ref.	Debit	Credit
20X8				
Oct. 26	Cash		2,625	
	Notes Receivable			2,500
	Interest Revenue			125
	Collect note–D. Brown			

If some of the interest has already been accrued (through adjusting entries that debited interest receivable and credited interest revenue), then the previously accrued interest is credited to interest receivable and the remainder of the interest is credited to interest revenue.

When the maker of a promissory note fails to pay, the note is said to be dishonored. The dishonored note may be recorded in one of two ways, depending upon whether or not the payee expects to collect the debt. If payment is expected, the company transfers the principal and interest to accounts receivable, removes the face value of the note from notes receivable, and recognizes the interest revenue. Assuming D. Brown dishonors the note but payment is expected, the company records the event by debiting accounts receivable from D. Brown for

$2,625, crediting notes receivable for $2,500, and crediting interest revenue for $125.

		General Journal			GJ42
Date	Account Title and Description	Ref.	Debit	Credit
20X8				
Oct. 26	Accounts Receivable–D. Brown		2,625	
	Notes Receivable			2,500
	Interest Revenue			125
	Dishonor note–D. Brown			

If D. Brown dishonors the note and the company believes the note is a bad debt, allowance for bad debts is debited for $2,500 and notes receivable is credited for $2,500. No interest revenue is recognized because none will ever be received.

		General Journal			GJ42
Date	Account Title and Description	Ref.	Debit	Credit
20X8				
Oct. 26	Allowance for Bad Debts		2,500	
	Notes Receivable			2,500
	Uncollectible note–D. Brown			

If interest on a bad debt had previously been accrued, then a correcting entry is needed to remove the accrued interest from interest revenue and interest receivable (by debiting interest revenue and crediting interest receivable). Although interest revenue would have been overstated in the accounting periods when the interest was accrued and would be understated in the period when the correcting entry occurs, efforts to amend prior statements or recognize the error in footnotes on forthcoming statements are not necessary except in rare situations where the bad debt changes reported revenue so much that the judgment of those who use financial statements is materially affected by the disclosure.

Discounting Notes Receivable

Just as accounts receivable can be factored, notes can be converted into cash by selling them to a financial institution at a discount. Notes are usually sold (discounted) with recourse, which means the company discounting the note agrees to pay the financial institution if the maker dishonors the note. When notes receivable are sold with recourse, the company has a contingent liability that must be disclosed in the notes accompanying the financial statements. A **contingent liability** is an obligation to pay an amount in the future, if and when an uncertain event occurs.

The **discount rate** is the annual percentage rate that the financial institution charges for buying a note and collecting the debt. The **discount period** is the length of time between a note's sale and its due date. The **discount,** which is the fee that the financial institution charges, is found by multiplying the note's maturity value by the discount rate and the discount period.

$$\text{Maturity Value of Note} \times \text{Discount Rate} \times \text{Discount Period} = \text{Discount}$$

Suppose a company accepts a 90-day, 9%, $5,000 note, which has a maturity value (principal + interest) of $5,110.96. In this example, precise calculations are made by using a 365-day year and by rounding results to the nearest penny.

Principal	$5,000.00
Interest ($5,000 \times .09 \times \dfrac{90}{365}$)	110.96
Maturity Value	$5,110.96

If the company immediately discounts with recourse the note to a bank that offers a 15% discount rate, the bank's discount is $189.04.

$$\$5,110.96 \times .15 \times \frac{90}{365} = \$189.04$$

The bank subtracts the discount from the note's maturity value and pays the company $4,921.92 for the note.

Maturity Value	$5,110.96
Discount	(189.04)
Discounted Value of Note	$4,921.92

The company determines the interest expense associated with this transaction by subtracting the discounted value of the note from the note's face value plus any interest revenue the company has earned from the note. Since the company discounts the note before earning any interest revenue, interest expense is $78.08 ($5000.00 – $4,921.92). The company records this transaction by debiting cash for $4,921.92, debiting interest expense for $78.08, and crediting notes receivable for $5,000.00.

General Journal				GJ23
Date	Account Title and Description	Ref.	Debit	Credit
20X1				
Jan. 15	Cash		4921.92	
	Interest Expense		78.08	
	Notes Receivable			5,000.00
	Discounted note to bank			

Suppose the company holds the note for 60 days before discounting it. After 60 days, the company has earned interest revenue of $73.97.

$$\$5,000.00 \ \times \ .09 \ \times \ \frac{60}{365} \ = \ \$73.97$$

Since the note's due date is 30 days away, the bank's discount is $63.01. The bank subtracts the discount from the note's maturity value and pays the company $5,047.95 for the note.

$$\text{Discount} = \$5,110.96 \times .15 \times \frac{30}{365} = \$63.01$$

Maturity Value	$5,110.96
Discount	(63.01)
Discounted Value of Note	$5,047.95

The company subtracts the discounted value of the note from the note's face value plus the interest revenue the company has earned from the note to determine the interest expense, if any, associated with discounting the note. In this example, the interest expense equals $26.02.

Note's Face Value + Interest Revenue Earned	$5,073.97
Discounted Value of Note	(5,047.95)
Interest Expense	$ 26.02

The company records this transaction by debiting cash for $5,047.95, debiting interest expense for $26.02, crediting notes receivable for $5,000.00, and crediting interest revenue for $73.97.

General Journal				GJ23
Date	Account Title and Description	Ref.	Debit	Credit
20X1				
Mar. 16	Cash		5047.95	
	Interest Expense		26.02	
	Notes Receivable			5,000.00
	Interest Revenue			73.97
	Discounted note to bank			

Merchandising and manufacturing companies keep an **inventory** of goods held for sale. Management is responsible for determining and maintaining the proper level of goods in inventory. If inventory contains too few items, sales may be missed. If inventory contains too many items, the business pays unnecessary amounts to warehouse, secure, and insure the items, and the company's cash flow becomes one sided—cash flows out to purchase inventory but cash does not flow in from sales.

Merchandising companies classify all goods available for sale in one inventory category. Manufacturing companies generally use three inventory categories: finished products, work in process, and raw materials. This chapter focuses on inventory for merchandising companies, but many of the principles and practices that are discussed apply to manufacturing companies as well. *Cliffs Quick Review Accounting Principles II* explains inventory accounting for manufacturing companies.

Determining Quantities of Merchandise in Inventory

Companies take **physical inventories** to count how many (or measure how much) of each item the company owns. Inventory is easier to count when sales and deliveries are not occurring, so many companies take inventory when the business is closed.

Taking a physical inventory involves the same types of internal control principles discussed in the first chapter of this book and in the chapter entitled "Cash." Some examples of these internal control principles appear below.

- **Segregation of duties.** Specific items should be counted by employees who do not have custody of the items.

- **Proper authorization.** Managers are responsible for assigning each employee to a specific set of inventory tasks. In addition, employees who help take inventory are responsible for verifying the contents of boxes, barrels, and other containers.

- **Adequate documents and records.** Prenumbered count sheets are provided to all employees involved in taking inventory. These count sheets provide evidence to support reported inventory levels and, when signed, show exactly who is responsible for the information they include.

- **Physical controls.** Access to inventory should be limited until the physical inventory is completed. If the company plans to ship inventory items during a physical inventory, these items should be placed in a separate area. Similarly, if the company receives inventory items during a physical inventory, these items should be kept in a designated area and counted separately.

- **Independent checks on performance.** After the employees finish counting, a supervisor should verify that all items have been counted and that none have been counted twice. Some companies use a second counter to check the first counter's results.

Consigned merchandise. Consigned merchandise is merchandise sold on behalf of another company or individual, who retains title to it. Although the seller (consignee) of the merchandise displays the items, only the owner (consignor) includes the items in inventory. Therefore, companies that sell goods on consignment must be careful to exclude from inventory those items provided by consignors.

Goods in transit. Goods in transit must be included in either the seller's or the buyer's inventory. When merchandise is shipped **FOB (free on board) shipping point,** the purchaser pays the shipping fees and gains title to the merchandise once it is shipped. Therefore, the merchandise must be included in the purchaser's inventory even if the purchaser has not yet received it. When merchandise is shipped **FOB (free on board) destination,** the seller pays the shipping fees and maintains title until the merchandise reaches the purchaser's place of business. Such merchandise must be included in the seller's inventory until the purchaser receives it. In addition to counting merchandise on hand, therefore, someone must examine the freight terms and shipping and receiving documents on purchases and sales just before and just after the count takes place to establish a more complete and accurate inventory count.

The Cost of Inventory

The cost of inventory includes the cost of purchased merchandise, less discounts that are taken, plus any duties and transportation costs paid by the purchaser. If the merchandise must be assembled or otherwise prepared for sale, then the cost of getting the product ready for sale is considered part of the cost of inventory. Technically, inventory costs include warehousing and insurance expenses associated with storing unsold merchandise. However, the cost of tracking this information often outweighs the benefits of allocating these costs to each unit of inventory, so many companies simply apply these costs directly to the cost of goods sold as the expenses are incurred.

The Valuation of Merchandise

To ensure the proper matching of expenses and revenues, decreases in the value of inventory due to usage, damage, deterioration, obsolescence, and other factors must be recognized in the accounting period during which the decrease occurs rather than the period during which the merchandise sells. Inventory should never be valued at more than its **net realizable value,** which equals its expected sales price minus any associated selling expenses. For example, if a storm damages a car that cost an automobile dealer $25,000, and if the car can now be sold for no more than $23,000, then the value of the car must be reported at $23,000. This decrease in the value of inventory is recognized by debiting the loss on inventory write-down account, which is an expense account, and by crediting inventory.

General Journal				GJ11
Date	Account Title and Description	Ref.	Debit	Credit
20X5				
Jun. 30	Loss on Inventory Write-Down	525	2,000	
	Inventory	125		2,000
	Write down car's value			

Loss on Inventory Write-Down					525
Date	Explanation	Ref.	Debit	Credit	Balance
20X5					
Jun. 30	Write down car's value	GJ11	2,000		2,000

Inventory					125
Date	Explanation	Ref.	Debit	Credit	Balance
20X5					896,000
Jun. 30	Write down car's value	GJ11		2,000	894,000

Some companies attribute inventory write-downs directly to the cost of goods sold, and some companies use other expense accounts for this purpose, so write-downs are not usually identified separately on financial statements.

Market value generally equals the replacement cost of inventory. Items sometimes decrease in value because they become less expensive to purchase. In other words, the market value drops. The **lower-of-cost-or-market (LCM) rule** is used to determine the value of merchandise inventory.

Suppose a retail computer store purchases one hundred computers for $3,000 each. After the store sells fifty of them, the manufacturer decreases the computer's price, enabling the store—as well as the store's competitors—to purchase the same type of computer for $2,500. Applying the lower-of-cost-or-market rule means the value of the fifty remaining computers equals $125,000 (50 × $2,500) rather than $150,000 (50 × $3,000). This $25,000 write-down is recorded by debiting the loss on inventory write-down account and by crediting inventory.

General Journal   GJ64

Date	Account Title and Description	Ref.	Debit	Credit
20X5				
Aug. 30	Loss on Inventory Write-Down	525	25,000	
	Inventory	125		25,000
	Write down computers			

Loss on Inventory Write-Down   525

Date	Explanation	Ref.	Debit	Credit	Balance
20X5					
Aug. 30	Write down computers	GJ64	25,000		25,000

Inventory   125

Date	Explanation	Ref.	Debit	Credit	Balance
20X5					481,000
Aug. 30	Write down computers	GJ64		25,000	456,000

Again, many companies choose to record write-downs using a different expense account than the one shown above.

The LCM rule may be applied to individual inventory items, to groups of similar items, or if the inventory consists of related items, to the entire inventory. As the chart below indicates, applying the LCM rule to individual items produces the most conservative valuation of inventory. As the number of items grouped together increases, the reported value of inventory tends to increase because increases in the market value of some items may partially offset decreases in the market value of other items in the same group.

	Cost	Market	LCM Rule applied to Items	LCM Rule applied to Groups	LCM Rule applied to Entire Inventory
Computers					
Model EX7	$150,000	$125,000	$125,000		
Model NX8	30,000	32,000	30,000		
Model VX9	50,000	55,000	50,000		
Total	230,000	212,000		$212,000	
Printers					
Model PL30	30,000	34,000	30,000		
Model PL60	15,000	18,000	15,000		
Model PL90	25,000	24,000	24,000		
Total	70,000	76,000		70,000	
Total inventory	$300,000	$288,000	$274,000	$282,000	$288,000

After the value of inventory has been written down, an increase in net realizable value or market value is not recorded. Instead, such increases are recognized as revenue when sales actually occur. Because companies must estimate net realizable value and because applying the LCM rule to individual items or groups of items yields different inventory values, financial statements should disclose the company's basis for determining the value of inventory.

Comparing Perpetual and Periodic Inventory Systems

Companies may use either the perpetual system or the periodic system to account for inventory. Under the **periodic system,** merchandise purchases are recorded in the purchases account, and the inventory account balance is updated only at the end of each accounting period. The chapter entitled "Accounting for a Merchandising Company," which begins on page 85, describes the periodic system in detail. Perpetual inventory systems have traditionally been associated with companies that sell small numbers of high-priced items, but the development of modern scanning and computer technology has enabled almost any type of merchandiser to consider using this system.

Under the **perpetual system,** purchases, purchase returns and allowances, purchase discounts, sales, and sales returns are immediately recognized in the inventory account, so the inventory account balance should always remain accurate, assuming there is no theft, spoilage, or other losses. Consider several entries under both systems. The reference columns are removed from the illustration to save space.

Periodic Method

General Journal   GJ11

Date	Accounts/Description	Dr.	Cr.
20X5			
Apr. 1	Purchases	800	
	AP–ACME		800
	Buy eight tires/$100 each		
4	AP–ACME	100	
	Purchases Returns		
	& Allowances		100
	Return one tire to ACME		
10	AP–ACME	700	
	Cash		686
	Purchases Discounts		14
	Pay for seven tires		
22	AR–M. Guittar	300	
	Sales		300
	Sell two tires/$150 each		
24	Sales Returns & Allow.	150	
	AR–M. Guittar		150
	Return of one tire		
30	Cash	150	
	AR–M. Guittar		150
	Payment from M. Guittar		

Perpetual Method

General Journal   GJ11

Date	Accounts/Description	Dr.	Cr.
20X5			
Apr. 1	Inventory–Tires	800	
	AP–ACME		800
	Buy eight tires/$100 each		
4	AP–ACME	100	
	Inventory–Tires		100
	Return one tire to ACME		
10	AP–ACME	700	
	Cash		686
	Inventory–Tires		14
	Pay for seven tires		
22	AR–M. Guittar	300	
	Sales		300
	Sell two tires/$150 each		
22	Cost of Goods Sold	200	
	Inventory–Tires		200
	Cost of tires/$100 each		
24	Sales Returns & Allow.	150	
	AR–M. Guittar		150
	Return of one tire		
24	Inventory–Tires	100	
	Cost of Goods Sold		100
	Add return to inventory		
30	Cash	150	
	AR–M. Guittar		150
	Payment from M. Guittar		

Note: AP stands for accounts payable, and AR stands for accounts receivable.

As the two sets of circled entries on the previous page indicate, two things happen when there is a sale or a sales return. First, the sales transaction's effect on revenue must be recognized by making an entry to increase accounts receivable and the sales account. Second, the flow of merchandise between inventory (an asset) and cost of goods sold (an expense) is recorded in accordance with the matching principle. A sales return has the opposite effect on the same accounts. Under the periodic system, the inventory and cost of goods sold accounts are updated only periodically, but under the perpetual system, entries that recognize a transaction's effect on these accounts occur when the revenue from the sale is recognized.

For convenience, a sale or sales return can be recorded under the perpetual system with a compound entry that lists all four accounts.

General Journal   GJ11

Date	Account Title and Description	Ref.	Debit	Credit
20X5				
Apr. 22	Accounts Receivable–M. Guittar	AR94	300	
	Cost of Goods Sold	560	200	
	Sales	400		300
	Inventory–Tires	I-635		200
	Sell two tires for $300 (cost of tires = $200)			

See pages 105–107 to review some background information about special journals and the sales journal. Textbooks almost always use a general journal to explain inventory accounting because the general journal provides a simple, consistent format to present new information. However, most companies would record the sale in a sales journal.

Inventory Subsidiary Ledger Accounts

Companies that use the perpetual system maintain an inventory control account and an inventory subsidiary ledger with separate accounts for each type of item the business sells. Whenever a transaction affects inventory, the specific item's subsidiary ledger account is also updated. Inventory subsidiary ledger accounts usually contain separate sets of columns for purchases, sales, and the account balance. Each set has three columns, which are used to record the number of units, the cost of each unit, and the total cost. The inventory–tires account from the previous example appears below.

Inventory–Tires   I-635

Max. 15 Min. 7		Purchases			Sales			Overall Balance		
Date	Description	Ref.	Units	Cost	Total	Units	Cost	Total	Units	Cost	Total
Apr. 1	Beginning inventory								7	$100	$ 700
1	Purchase	GJ1	8	$100	$800				15	100	1,500
4	Purchase return	GJ1	(1)	(100)	(100)				14	100	1,400
10	Purchase discount	GJ1			(2)	(14)			14	99	1,386
22	Sale	GJ1				2	99	198	12	99	1,188
24	Sales return	GJ1				1	(99)	(99)	13	99	1,287

The numbers in the maximum and minimum fields near the upper left corner of the account are optional control fields designed to prevent the company from having too many or too few of the items in stock. In this example, the company purchases new tires whenever the overall number of units in stock drops to seven or less, and the number purchased should never cause the company's stock to exceed fifteen units.

If you study the journal entries on page 159 and the subsidiary ledger account above, you will notice that the cost of the tires sold on April 22 changes from $100 in the journal entries to $99 in the inventory account. These examples illustrate two different cost flow methods, so they are intended to be used for illustration purposes only. A company must use one cost flow method consistently. The next section of this chapter explains in detail the methods that companies use to determine the cost of goods sold.

Cost Flow Methods

The cost of items remaining in inventory and the cost of goods sold are easy to determine if purchase prices and other inventory costs never change, but price fluctuations may force a company to make certain assumptions about which items have sold and which items remain in inventory. There are four generally accepted methods for assigning costs to ending inventory and cost of goods sold: specific cost; average cost; first-in, first-out (FIFO); and last-in, first-out (LIFO). On the next several pages, each method is applied to the information below, which summarizes the activity in one inventory subsidiary ledger account at a company named Zapp Electronics.

January 1	Beginning inventory—100 units @ $14/unit
March 20	Sale of 50 units
April 10	Purchase of 150 units @ $16/unit
July 15	Sale of 100 units
September 30	Sale of 50 units
October 10	Purchase of 200 units @ $17/unit
December 15	Sale of 150 units
December 31	Ending inventory—100 units

The cost of goods available for sale equals the beginning value of inventory plus the cost of goods purchased. Two purchases occurred during the year, so the cost of goods available for sale is $7,200.

	Units		Per Unit Cost		Total Cost
Beginning Inventory	100	×	$14	=	$1,400
+ Purchase—April 10	150	×	$16	=	2,400
+ Purchase—October 10	200	×	$17	=	3,400
= Cost of Goods Available for Sale	450				$7,200

Specific cost. Companies can use the specific cost method only when the purchase date and cost of each unit in inventory is identifiable. For the most part, companies that use this method sell a small number of expensive items, such as automobiles or appliances.

If specially coded price tags or some other technique enables Zapp Electronics to determine that 15 units in ending inventory were purchased on April 10 and the remaining 85 units were purchased on October 10, then the ending value of inventory and the cost of goods sold can be determined precisely.

	Units	Per Unit Cost	Total Cost
Purchased April 10	15 ×	$16 =	$ 240
Purchased October 10	85 ×	$17 =	1,445
Ending Inventory	100		$1,685

Cost of Goods Available for Sale	$7,200
– Ending Inventory	(1,685)
= Cost of Goods Sold	$5,515

Since the specific cost of each unit is known, the resulting values for ending inventory and cost of goods sold are not affected by whether the company uses a periodic or perpetual system to account for inventory. The only difference between the systems is that the value of inventory and the cost of goods sold is determined every time a sale occurs under the perpetual system, and these amounts are calculated at the end of the accounting period under the periodic system. Check the value found for cost of goods sold by multiplying the 350 units that sold by their per unit cost.

	Units	Per Unit Cost	Total Cost
Beginning Inventory	100 ×	$14 =	$1,400
Purchased April 10	135 ×	$16 =	2,160
Purchased October 10	115 ×	$17 =	1,955
Cost of Goods Sold	350		$5,515

Companies that sell a large number of inexpensive items generally do not track the specific cost of each unit in inventory. Instead, they use one of the other three methods to allocate inventoriable costs. These other methods (average cost, FIFO, and LIFO) are built upon certain assumptions about how merchandise flows through the company, so they are often referred to as **assumed cost flow methods** or **cost flow assumptions.** Accounting principles do not require companies to choose a cost flow method that approximates the actual movement of inventory items.

Average cost. Companies that use the periodic system and want to apply the same cost to all units in an inventory account use the **weighted average cost method.** The weighted average cost per unit equals the cost of goods available for sale divided by the number of units available for sale.

For Zapp Electronics, the cost of goods available for sale is $7,200 and the number of units available for sale is 450, so the weighted average cost per unit is $16.

$$\frac{\$7,200}{450} = \$16$$

The weighted average cost per unit multiplied by the number of units remaining in inventory determines the ending value of inventory. Subtracting this amount from the cost of goods available for sale equals the cost of goods sold.

Cost of Goods Available for Sale	$7,200
− Ending Inventory (100 × $16)	(1,600)
= Cost of Goods Sold	$5,600

Check the value found for cost of goods sold by multiplying the 350 units that sold by the weighted average cost per unit.

Cost of Goods Sold (350 × $16) = $5,600

Companies that use the perpetual system and want to apply the average cost to all units in an inventory account use the **moving average method.** Every time a purchase occurs under this method, a new weighted average cost per unit is calculated and applied to the items.

As the chart below indicates, the moving average cost per unit changes from $14.00 to $15.50 after the purchase on April 10 and becomes $16.70 after the purchase on October 10.

Date	Purchases	Sales	Balance
Jan. 1			100 @ $14.00 = $1,400
Mar. 20		50 @ $14.00 = $ 700	50 @ $14.00 = $ 700
Apr. 10	150 @ $16.00 = $2,400		200 @ $15.50 = $3,100
July 15		100 @ $15.50 = $1,550	100 @ $15.50 = $1,550
Sep. 30		50 @ $15.50 = $ 775	50 @ $15.50 = $ 775
Oct. 10	200 @ $17.00 = $3,400		250 @ $16.70 = $4,175
Dec. 15		150 @ $16.70 = $2,505	100 @ $16.70 = $1,670

Use the final moving average cost per unit to calculate the ending value of inventory and the cost of goods sold.

Cost of Goods Available for Sale	$7,200
– Ending Inventory (100 × $16.70)	(1,670)
= Cost of Goods Sold	$5,530

First-in, first-out. The first-in, first-out (FIFO) method assumes the first units purchased are the first to be sold. In other words, the last units purchased are always the ones remaining in inventory. Using this method, Zapp Electronics assumes that all 100 units in ending inventory were purchased on October 10.

Cost of Goods Available for Sale	$7,200
– Ending Inventory (100 × $17)	(1,700)
= Cost of Goods Sold	$5,500

Check the value found for cost of goods sold by multiplying the 350 units that sold by their per unit cost.

	Units	Per Unit Cost	Total Cost
Beginning Inventory	100 ×	$14 =	$1,400
Purchased April 10	150 ×	$16 =	2,400
Purchased October 10	100 ×	$17 =	1,700
Cost of Goods Sold	350		$5,500

The first-in, first-out method yields the same result whether the company uses a periodic or perpetual system. Under the perpetual system, the first-in, first-out method is applied at the time of sale. The earliest purchases on hand at the time of sale are assumed to be sold.

Date	Purchases	Sales	Balance
Jan. 1			100 @ $14.00 = $1,400
Mar. 20		50 @ $14.00 = $ 700	50 @ $14.00 = $ 700
Apr. 10	150 @ $16.00 = $2,400		50 @ $14.00 } $3,100 150 @ $16.00
July 15		50 @ $14.00 } $1,500 50 @ $16.00	100 @ $16.00 = $1,600
Sep. 30		50 @ $16.00 = $ 800	50 @ $16.00 = $ 800
Oct. 10	200 @ $17.00 = $3,400		50 @ $16.00 } $4,200 200 @ $17.00
Dec. 15		50 @ $16.00 } $2,500 100 @ $17.00	100 @ $17.00 = $1,700

Last-in, first-out. The last-in, first-out (LIFO) method assumes the last units purchased are the first to be sold. Therefore, the first units purchased always remain in inventory. This method usually produces different results depending on whether the company uses a periodic or perpetual system.

If Zapp Electronics uses the last-in, first-out method with a periodic system, the 100 units remaining at the end of the period are assumed to be the same 100 units in beginning inventory.

Cost of Goods Available for Sale	$7,200
− Ending Inventory (100 × $14)	(1,400)
= Cost of Goods Sold	$5,800

Check the value found for cost of goods sold by multiplying the 350 units that sold by their per unit cost.

	Units	Per Unit Cost	Total Cost
Purchased October 10	200 ×	$17 =	$3,400
Purchased April 10	150 ×	$16 =	2,400
Cost of Goods Sold	350		$5,800

If Zapp Electronics uses the last-in, first-out method with a perpetual system, the cost of the last units purchased is allocated to cost of goods sold whenever a sale occurs. Therefore, the assumption would be that the 50 units sold on March 20 came from beginning inventory, the units sold on July 15 and September 30 were all purchased on April 10, and the units sold on December 15 were all purchased on October 10. Therefore ending inventory consists of 50 units from beginning inventory and 50 units from the October 10 purchase.

Date	Purchases	Sales	Balance
Jan. 1			100 @ $14.00 = $1,400
Mar. 20		50 @ $14.00 = $ 700	50 @ $14.00 = $ 700
Apr. 10	150 @ $16.00 = $2,400		50 @ $14.00 150 @ $16.00 } $3,100
July 15		100 @ $16.00 = $1,600	50 @ $14.00 50 @ $16.00 } $1,500
Sep. 30		50 @ $16.00 = $ 800	50 @ $14.00 = $ 700
Oct. 10	200 @ $17.00 = $3,400		50 @ $14.00 200 @ $17.00 } $4,100
Dec. 15		150 @ $17.00 = $2,550	50 @ $14.00 50 @ $17.00 } $1,550

	Units	Per Unit Cost	Total Cost
Beginning Inventory	50	× $14 =	$ 700
Purchased October 10	50	× $17 =	850
Ending Inventory	100		$1,550

Cost of Goods Available for Sale	$7,200
– Ending Inventory	(1,550)
= Cost of Goods Sold	$5,650

Check the value found for cost of goods sold by multiplying the 350 units that sold by their per unit cost.

	Units	Per Unit Cost	Total Cost
Beginning Inventory	50 ×	$14 =	$ 700
Purchased April 10	150 ×	$16 =	2,400
Purchased October 10	150 ×	$17 =	2,550
Cost of Goods Sold	350		$5,650

Comparing the assumed cost flow methods. Although the cost of goods available for sale is the same under each cost flow method, each method allocates costs to ending inventory and cost of goods sold differently. Compare the values found for ending inventory and cost of goods sold under the various assumed cost flow methods in the previous examples.

	Weighted Average (Periodic)	Moving Average (Perpetual)	FIFO (Periodic or Perpetual)	LIFO (Periodic)	LIFO (Perpetual)
Ending Inventory	$1,600	$1,670	$1,700	$1,400	$1,550
Cost of Goods Sold	5,600	5,530	5,500	5,800	5,650
Cost of Goods Available for Sale	$7,200	$7,200	$7,200	$7,200	$7,200

If the cost of goods sold varies, net income varies. Less net income means a smaller tax bill. In times of rising prices, LIFO (especially LIFO in a periodic system) produces the lowest ending inventory value, the highest cost of goods sold, and the lowest net income. Therefore, many companies in the United States use LIFO even if the method does not accurately reflect the actual flow of merchandise through the company. The Internal Revenue Service accepts LIFO as long as the same method is used for financial reporting purposes.

The Effect of Inventory Errors on Financial Statements

Income statement effects. An incorrect inventory balance causes an error in the calculation of cost of goods sold and, therefore, an error in the calculation of gross profit and net income. Left unchanged, the error has the opposite effect on cost of goods sold, gross profit, and net income in the following accounting period because the first accounting period's ending inventory is the second period's beginning inventory. The total cost of goods sold, gross profit, and net income for the two periods will be correct, but the allocation of these amounts between periods will be incorrect. Since financial statement users depend upon accurate statements, care must be taken to ensure that the inventory balance at the end of each accounting period is correct. The chart below identifies the effect that an incorrect inventory balance has on the income statement.

Error in Inventory	Impact of Error on		
	Cost of Goods Sold	Gross Profit	Net Income
Ending Inventory			
Understated	Overstated	Understated	Understated
Overstated	Understated	Overstated	Overstated
Beginning Inventory			
Understated	Understated	Overstated	Overstated
Overstated	Overstated	Understated	Understated

Balance sheet effects. An incorrect inventory balance causes the reported value of assets and owner's equity on the balance sheet to be wrong. This error does not affect the balance sheet in the following accounting period, assuming the company accurately determines the inventory balance for that period.

Error in Inventory	Impact of Error on		
	Assets =	Liabilities +	Owner's Equity
Understated	Understated	No Effect	Understated
Overstated	Overstated	No Effect	Overstated

Estimating Inventories

Companies sometimes need to determine the value of inventory when a physical count is impossible or impractical. For example, a company may need to know how much inventory was destroyed in a fire. Companies using the perpetual system simply report the inventory account balance in such situations, but companies using the periodic system must estimate the value of inventory. Two ways of estimating inventory levels are the gross profit method and the retail inventory method.

Gross profit method. The gross profit method estimates the value of inventory by applying the company's historical gross profit percentage to current-period information about net sales and the cost of goods available for sale. **Gross profit** equals net sales minus the cost of goods sold. The **gross profit margin** equals gross profit divided by net sales. If a company had net sales of $4,000,000 during the previous year and the cost of goods sold during that year was $2,600,000, then gross profit was $1,400,000 and the gross profit margin was 35%.

Net Sales	$4,000,000
Less: Cost of Goods Sold	(2,600,000)
Gross Profit	$1,400,000

$$\text{Gross Profit Margin } = \frac{\$1,400,000}{\$4,000,000} = 35\%$$

If gross profit margin is 35%, then cost of goods sold is 65% of net sales.

Suppose that one month into the current fiscal year, the company decides to use the gross profit margin from the previous year to estimate inventory. Net sales for the month were $500,000, beginning inventory was $50,000, and purchases during the month totaled $300,000. First, the company multiplies net sales for the month by the historical gross profit margin to estimate gross profit.

Net Sales × Gross Profit Margin = Gross Profit

$500,000 × 35% = $175,000

Next, estimated gross profit is subtracted from net sales to estimate the cost of goods sold.

Net Sales	$500,000
Gross Profit	(175,000)
Cost of Goods Sold	$325,000

Alternatively, cost of goods sold may be determined by multiplying net sales by 65% (100% − gross profit margin of 35%).

Finally, the estimated cost of goods sold is subtracted from the cost of goods available for sale to estimate the value of inventory.

Beginning Inventory	$ 50,000
Purchases	300,000
Cost of Goods Available for Sale	350,000
Less: Cost of Goods Sold	(325,000)
Ending Inventory	$ 25,000

The gross profit method produces a reasonably accurate result as long as the historical gross profit margin still applies to the current period. However, increasing competition, new market conditions, and other factors may cause the historical gross profit margin to change over time.

Retail inventory method. Retail businesses track both the cost and retail sales price of inventory. This information provides another way to estimate ending inventory. Suppose a retail store wants to estimate the cost of ending inventory using the information shown below.

	Cost	Retail
Beginning Inventory	$ 49,000	$ 80,000
Purchases	209,000	350,000
Goods Available for Sale	$258,000	430,000
Net Sales		$400,000

The first step is to calculate the retail value of ending inventory by subtracting net sales from the retail value of goods available for sale.

	Cost	Retail
Beginning Inventory	$ 49,000	$ 80,000
Purchases	209,000	350,000
Goods Available for Sale	$258,000	430,000
Net Sales		400,000
Ending Inventory (Retail)		$ 30,000

Next, the cost-to-retail ratio is calculated by dividing the cost of goods available for sale by the retail value of goods available for sale.

	Cost	Retail
Beginning Inventory	$ 49,000	$ 80,000
Purchases	209,000	350,000
Goods Available for Sale	$258,000	430,000
Net Sales		400,000
Ending Inventory (Retail)		$ 30,000
Cost to Retail Ratio		
($258,000 ÷ $430,000 = 60%)		

Then, the estimated cost of ending inventory is found by multiplying the retail value of ending inventory by the cost-to-retail ratio.

	Cost	Retail
Beginning Inventory	$ 49,000	$ 80,000
Purchases	209,000	350,000
Goods Available for Sale	$258,000	430,000
Net Sales		400,000
Ending Inventory (Retail)		$ 30,000
Cost to Retail Ratio ($258,000 ÷ $430,000 = 60%)		
Ending Inventory (Cost) ($30,000 × 60%)	$ 18,000	

One limitation of the retail inventory method is that a store's cost-to-retail ratio may vary significantly from one type of item to another, but the calculation simply uses an average ratio. If the items that actually sold have a cost-to-retail ratio that differs significantly from the ratio used in the calculation, the estimate will be inaccurate.

OPERATING ASSETS

Operating assets are long-lived assets that are used in normal business operations. They are not held for resale to customers. Investments in operating assets are essential to the success of most businesses. There are three major categories of operating assets: property, plant, and equipment, which is a category that some textbooks refer to as plant assets or fixed assets; natural resources; and intangible assets. **Property, plant, and equipment** includes land; land improvements, such as driveways, parking lots, fences, and similar items that require periodic repair and replacement; buildings; equipment; vehicles; and furniture. **Natural resources,** such as timber, fossil fuels, and mineral deposits, are created by natural processes that may take thousands or even millions of years to complete. Companies use up natural resources by cutting or extracting them, so natural resources are sometimes called **wasting assets. Intangible assets,** which lack physical substance, may nevertheless provide substantial value to a company. Patents, copyrights, and trademarks are examples of intangible assets.

According to the matching principle, the costs of operating assets other than land must be matched with the revenues they help to generate over their useful lives. Allocating these costs to expense is called depreciation for plant assets, depletion for natural resources, and amortization for intangible assets. The cost of land is never depreciated because land is considered to have an unlimited useful life.

Natural resources are usually listed within the property, plant, and equipment category on the balance sheet. Intangible assets are placed in a separate category.

Digby Pitts Strip Mining
Partial Balance Sheet
December 31, 20X4

ASSETS			
Current Assets			
Cash		$	16,000
Accounts Receivable			84,000
Inventory			189,000
Supplies			3,000
Prepaid Insurance			8,000
Total Current Assets			300,000
Property, Plant, and Equipment			
Land		$ 300,000	
Buildings and Equipment	$ 500,000		
Less: Accumulated Depreciation	(200,000)	300,000	
Coal Deposits	5,000,000		
Less: Accumulated Depletion	(2,000,000)	3,000,000	3,600,000
Intangible Assets			
Leaseholds		100,000	
Goodwill		400,000	
Less: Accumulated Amortization		(100,000)	400,000
Total Assets			$4,300,000

The Cost of Property, Plant, and Equipment

The cost of property, plant, and equipment includes the purchase price of the asset and all expenditures necessary to prepare the asset for its intended use.

Land. Land purchases often involve real estate commissions, legal fees, bank fees, title search fees, and similar expenses. To be prepared for use, land may need to be cleared of trees, drained and filled, graded to remove small hills and depressions, and landscaped. In addition, old buildings may need to be demolished before the company can use the land. Such demolition expenses are considered part of the land's cost. For example, if a company purchases land for $100,000, pays an additional $3,000 in closing costs, and pays $22,000 to have an old warehouse on the land demolished, then the company records the cost of the land at $125,000.

Land improvements. The cost of land improvements includes all expenditures associated with making the improvements ready for use. For example, when one business contracts with another business to put a parking lot on a piece of land, the cost of the parking lot is simply the agreed-upon price. A company that builds its own parking lot would determine the lot's cost by combining the cost of materials and wages paid to employees for building the lot.

Buildings. The cost of buildings includes the purchase price and all closing costs associated with the acquisition of the buildings, including payments by the purchaser for back taxes owed. Remodeling an acquired building and making repairs necessary for it to be used are also considered part of the cost. If a building is constructed for the company over an extended period, interest payments to finance the structure are included in the cost of the asset only while construction takes place. After construction is complete and the building is ready for productive use, interest payments are classified as interest expense.

Equipment, vehicles, and furniture. The cost of equipment, vehicles, and furniture includes the purchase price, sales taxes, transportation fees, insurance paid to cover the item during shipment, assembly, installation, and all other costs associated with making the item ready for use. These costs do not include such things as motor vehicle licensing and insurance, however, even if they are paid when a vehicle purchase occurs. Expenses of this type are normal, recurring operational expenses that do not add lasting value to the vehicle.

Depreciation

Depreciation is the process of allocating the cost of long-lived plant assets other than land to expense over the asset's estimated useful life. For financial reporting purposes, companies may choose from several different depreciation methods. Before studying some of the methods that companies use to depreciate assets, make sure you understand the definitions below.

> **Useful life** is an estimate of the productive life of an asset. Although usually expressed in years, an asset's useful life may also be based on units of activity, such as items produced, hours used, or miles driven.
>
> **Salvage value** equals the value, if any, that a company expects to receive by selling or exchanging an asset at the end of its useful life.
>
> **Depreciable cost** equals an asset's total cost minus the asset's expected salvage value. The total amount of depreciation expense assigned to an asset never exceeds the asset's depreciable cost.
>
> **Net book value** is an asset's total cost minus the accumulated depreciation assigned to the asset. Net book value rarely equals market value, which is the price someone would pay for the asset. In fact, the market value of an asset, such as a building, may increase while the asset is being depreciated. Net book value simply represents the portion of an asset's cost that has not been allocated to expense.

Straight-line depreciation. There are many depreciation methods available to companies. Straight-line depreciation, introduced on page 48, is the method that companies most frequently use for financial reporting purposes. If **straight-line depreciation** is used, an asset's annual depreciation expense is calculated by dividing the asset's depreciable cost by the number of years in the asset's useful life.

Calculating Straight-Line Depreciation

$$\frac{\text{Depreciable Cost}}{\text{Useful Life in Years}} = \text{Annual Depreciation Expense}$$

Another way to describe this calculation is to say that the asset's depreciable cost is multiplied by the **straight-line rate,** which equals one divided by the number of years in the asset's useful life.

Calculating Straight-Line Depreciation

$$\frac{1}{\text{Useful Life in Years}} = \text{Straight-Line Rate}$$

$$\text{Straight-Line Rate} \times \text{Depreciable Cost} = \text{Annual Depreciation Expense}$$

Suppose a company purchases a $90,000 truck and expects the truck to have a salvage value of $10,000 after five years. The depreciable cost of the truck is $80,000 ($90,000 – $10,000), and the asset's annual depreciation expense using straight-line depreciation is $16,000 ($80,000 ÷ 5).

Cost	$90,000
Less: Salvage Value	(10,000)
Depreciable Cost	$80,000

Calculating Straight-Line Depreciation

$$\frac{\$80,000}{5} = \$16,000 \quad \text{or:} \quad \frac{1}{5} = 20\%$$

$$20\% \times \$80,000 = \$16,000$$

The table below summarizes the application of straight-line depreciation during the truck's five-year useful life.

Straight-Line Depreciation

	Straight-Line Rate		Depreciable Cost		Annual Depreciation Expense	Accumulated Depreciation	Net Book Value
Cost							$90,000
Year 1	20%	×	$80,000	=	$16,000	$16,000	74,000
Year 2	20%	×	80,000	=	16,000	32,000	58,000
Year 3	20%	×	80,000	=	16,000	48,000	42,000
Year 4	20%	×	80,000	=	16,000	64,000	26,000
Year 5	20%	×	80,000	=	16,000	80,000	10,000

At the end of year five, the $80,000 shown as accumulated depreciation equals the asset's depreciable cost, and the $10,000 net book value represents its estimated salvage value.

To record depreciation expense on the truck each year, the company debits depreciation expense–vehicles for $16,000 and credits accumulated depreciation–vehicles for $16,000.

General Journal   GJ99

Date	Account Title and Description	Ref.	Debit	Credit
20X0				
Dec. 31	Depreciation Expense–Vehicles	556	16,000	
	Accumulated Depreciation–Vehicles	156		16,000
	Annual depreciation on truck			

Depreciation Expense–Vehicles   556

Date	Explanation	Ref.	Debit	Credit	Balance
20X0					
Dec. 31	Annual depreciation on truck	GJ99	16,000		16,000

Accumulated Depreciation–Vehicles   156

Date	Explanation	Ref.	Debit	Credit	Balance
20X0					
Dec. 31	Annual depreciation on truck	GJ99		16,000	16,000

If another depreciation method had been used, the accounts that appear in the entry would be the same, but the amounts would be different.

Companies use separate accumulated depreciation accounts for buildings, equipment, and other types of depreciable assets. Companies with a large number of depreciable assets may even create subsidiary ledger accounts to track the individual assets and the accumulated depreciation on each asset.

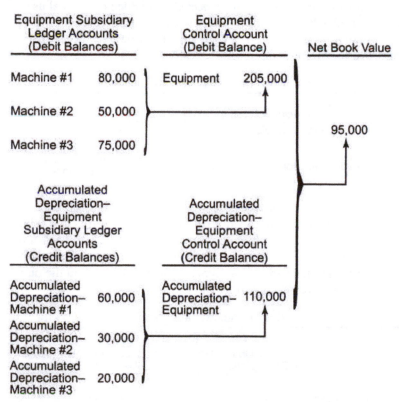

Units-of-activity depreciation. The useful life of some assets, particularly vehicles and equipment, is frequently determined by usage. For example, a toy manufacturer may expect a certain machine to produce one million dolls, or an airline may expect an airplane to provide ten thousand hours of flight time. **Units-of-activity depreciation,** which is sometimes called **units-of-production depreciation,** allocates the depreciable cost of an asset based on its usage. A per-unit cost of usage is found by dividing the asset's depreciable cost by the number of units the asset is expected to produce or by total usage as measured in hours or miles. The per-unit cost times the actual number of units in one year equals the amount of depreciation expense recorded for the asset that year.

Calculating Units-of-Activity Depreciation

$$\frac{\text{Depreciable Cost}}{\text{Units in Useful Life}} = \text{Per-Unit Depreciation}$$

$$\text{Per-Unit Depreciation} \times \text{Units During Year} = \text{Annual Depreciation Expense}$$

If a truck with a depreciable cost of $80,000 ($90,000 cost less $10,000 estimated salvage value) is expected to be driven 400,000 miles during its service life, the truck depreciates $0.20 each mile ($80,000 ÷ 400,000 miles = $0.20 per mile). The table below shows how depreciation expense is assigned to the truck based on the number of miles driven each year.

Units-of-Activity Depreciation

	Units (Miles)		Per-Unit Depreciation		Annual Depreciation Expense	Accumulated Depreciation	Net Book Value
Cost							$90,000
Year 1	110,000	×	$0.20	=	$22,000	$22,000	68,000
Year 2	70,000	×	0.20	=	14,000	36,000	54,000
Year 3	90,000	×	0.20	=	18,000	54,000	36,000
Year 4	80,000	×	0.20	=	16,000	70,000	20,000
Year 5	50,000	×	0.20	=	10,000	80,000	10,000

Sum-of-the-years'-digits depreciation. Equipment and vehicles often provide greater benefits when they are new than when they approach the end of their useful lives and more frequently require repairs. Using **sum-of-the-years'-digits depreciation** is one way for companies to assign a disproportionate share of depreciation expense to the first years of an asset's useful life. Under this method, depreciation expense is calculated using the equation shown below.

Calculating Sum-of-the-Years'-Digits Depreciation

$$\frac{\text{Years Remaining in the Asset's Useful Life at the Beginning of the Year}}{\text{Sum of the Years' Digits (explained below)}} \times \text{Depreciable Cost} = \frac{\text{Annual Depreciation}}{\text{Expense}}$$

The equation's denominator (the sum of the years' digits) can be found by adding each integer from one through the number of years in the asset's useful life $(1 + 2 + 3 \ldots)$ or by substituting the number of years in the asset's useful life for x in the equation below.

$$\frac{x(x + 1)}{2} = \text{Sum of the Years' Digits}$$

The sum of the years' digits for an asset with a five-year useful life is 15.

$$1 + 2 + 3 + 4 + 5 = 15 \quad \text{or} \quad \frac{5(5 + 1)}{2} = 15$$

Therefore, depreciation expense on the asset equals five-fifteenths of the depreciable cost during the first year, four-fifteenths during the second year, three-fifteenths during the third year, two-fifteenths during the fourth year, and one-fifteenth during the last year.

The table below shows how the sum-of-the-years'-digits method allocates depreciation expense to the truck, which has a depreciable cost of $80,000 ($90,000 cost less $10,000 expected salvage value) and a useful life of five years.

Sum-of-the-Years'-Digits Depreciation

	SYD Fraction		Depreciable Cost		Annual Depreciation Expense	Accumulated Depreciation	Net Book Value
Cost							$90,000
Year 1	$5/15$	×	$80,000	=	$26,667	$26,667	63,333
Year 2	$4/15$	×	80,000	=	21,333	48,000	42,000
Year 3	$3/15$	×	80,000	=	16,000	64,000	26,000
Year 4	$2/15$	×	80,000	=	10,667	74,667	15,333
Year 5	$1/15$	×	80,000	=	5,333	80,000	10,000

Declining-balance depreciation. Declining-balance depreciation provides another way for companies to shift a disproportionate amount of depreciation expense to the first years of an asset's useful life. **Declining-balance depreciation** is found by multiplying an asset's net book value (not its depreciable cost) by some multiple of the straight-line rate for the asset. The straight-line rate is one divided by the number of years in the asset's useful life. Companies typically use twice (200%) the straight-line rate, which is called the double-declining-balance rate, but rates of 125%, 150%, or 175% of the straight-line rate are also used. Once the declining-balance depreciation rate is determined, it stays the same for the asset's useful life.

Calculating Declining-Balance Depreciation

$$\frac{1}{\text{Useful Life in Years}} \times \frac{\text{Multiple}}{\text{(200\%, 175\%, 150\%, or 125\%)}} = \begin{array}{c}\text{Declining-Balance} \\ \text{Depreciation Rate} \\ \text{(DBD Rate)}\end{array}$$

$$\begin{array}{c}\text{Declining-Balance} \\ \text{Depreciation Rate} \\ \text{(DBD Rate)}\end{array} \times \begin{array}{c}\text{Beginning-of-Year} \\ \text{Net Book Value}\end{array} = \begin{array}{c}\text{Annual Depreciation} \\ \text{Expense}\end{array}$$

To illustrate double-declining-balance depreciation, consider the truck that has a cost of $90,000, an expected salvage value of $10,000, and a five-year useful life. The truck's net book value at acquisition is also $90,000 because no depreciation expense has been recorded yet. The straight-line rate for an asset with a five-year useful life is 20% (1 ÷ 5 = 20%), so the double-declining-balance rate, which uses the 200% multiple, is 40% (20% × 200% = 40%). The table below shows how the double-declining-balance method allocates depreciation expense to the truck.

Double-Declining-Balance Depreciation

	DBD Rate		Beginning-of-Year Book Value		Annual Depreciation Expense	Accumulated Depreciation	End-of-Year Book Value
Year 1	40%	×	$90,000	=	$36,000	$36,000	$54,000
Year 2	40%	×	54,000	=	21,600	57,600	32,400
Year 3	40%	×	32,400	=	12,960	70,560	19,440
Year 4	40%	×	19,440	=	7,776	78,336	11,664
Year 5	40%	×	11,664		1,664*	80,000	10,000

* Limited to $1,664 so book value does not go below salvage value.

At the end of an asset's useful life, the asset's net book value should equal its salvage value. Although 40% of $11,664 is $4,666, the truck depreciates only $1,664 during year five because net book value must never drop below salvage value. If the truck's salvage value were $5,000, depreciation expense during year five would have been $6,664. If the truck's salvage value were $20,000, then depreciation expense would have been limited to $12,400 during year three, and no depreciation expense would be recorded during year four or year five.

Comparing depreciation methods. All depreciation methods are designed to systematically allocate the depreciable cost of an asset to expense during the asset's useful life. Although total depreciation expense is the same no matter what depreciation method is used, the methods differ from each other in the specific assignment of depreciation expense to each year or accounting period. Consider how the depreciation methods discussed on the last several pages have assigned the truck's depreciable cost of $80,000 to depreciation expense over five years.

| | Annual Depreciation Expense | | | |
	Straight-Line Depreciation	Units-of-Activity Depreciation	Sum-of-the-Years'-Digits Depreciation	Double-Declining-Balance Depreciation
Year 1	$16,000	$22,000	$26,667	$36,000
Year 2	16,000	14,000	21,333	21,600
Year 3	16,000	18,000	16,000	12,960
Year 4	16,000	16,000	10,667	7,776
Year 5	16,000	10,000	5,333	1,664
	$80,000	$80,000	$80,000	$80,000

The sum-of-the-years'-digits and double-declining-balance methods are called accelerated depreciation methods because they allocate more depreciation expense to the first few years of an asset's life than to its later years.

Partial-year depreciation calculations. Partial-year depreciation expense calculations are necessary when depreciable assets are purchased, retired, or sold in the middle of an annual accounting period or when the company produces quarterly or monthly financial statements. The units-of-activity method is unaffected by partial-year depreciation calculations because the per-unit depreciation expense is simply multiplied by the number of units actually used during the period in question. For all other depreciation methods, however, annual depreciation expense is multiplied by a fraction that has the number of months the asset depreciates as its numerator and twelve as its denominator. Since depreciation expense calculations are estimates to begin with, rounding the time period to the nearest month is acceptable for financial reporting purposes.

Suppose the truck is purchased on July 26 and the company's annual accounting period ends on December 31. The company must record five months of depreciation expense on December 31 (August–December).

Under the straight-line method, the first full year's annual depreciation expense of $16,000 is multiplied by five-twelfths to calculate depreciation expense for the truck's first five months of use. $16,000 of depreciation expense is assigned to the truck in each of the next four years, and seven months of depreciation expense is assigned to the truck in the following year.

Straight-Line Depreciation

	Straight-Line Rate		Depreciable Cost		Annual Depreciation Expense	Accumulated Depreciation	Net Book Value
Cost							$90,000
Year 1 (5 mo.)	$5/12 \times 20\%$	×	$80,000	=	$ 6,667	$ 6,667	83,333
Year 2	20%	×	80,000	=	16,000	22,667	67,333
Year 3	20%	×	80,000	=	16,000	38,667	51,333
Year 4	20%	×	80,000	=	16,000	54,667	35,333
Year 5	20%	×	80,000	=	16,000	70,667	19,333
Year 6 (7 mo.)	$7/12 \times 20\%$	×	80,000	=	9,333	80,000	10,000

Under the declining-balance method, the first full year's annual depreciation expense of $36,000 is multiplied by five-twelfths to calculate depreciation expense for the truck's first five months of use. In subsequent years, the truck's net book value is higher than it would have been if a full year's depreciation expense had been assigned during the first year, but the declining-balance method's calculation of depreciation expense is otherwise unchanged.

Double-Declining-Balance Depreciation

	DBD Rate		Beginning-of-Year Book Value		Annual Depreciation Expense	Accumulated Depreciation	End-of-Year Book Value
Year 1 (5 mo.)	$5/12 \times 40\%$	×	$90,000	=	$15,000	$15,000	$75,000
Year 2	40%	×	75,000	=	30,000	45,000	45,000
Year 3	40%	×	45,000	=	18,000	63,000	27,000
Year 4	40%	×	27,000	=	10,800	73,800	16,200
Year 5	40%	×	16,200		6,200*	80,000	10,000
Year 6 (7 mo.)					0	80,000	10,000

* Limited to $6,200 so book value does not go below salvage value.

Under the sum-of-the-years'-digits method, the first full year's annual depreciation expense of $26,667 is multiplied by five-twelfths to calculate depreciation expense for the truck's first five months of use. During the second year, depreciation expense is calculated in two steps. The remaining seven-twelfths of the first full year's annual depreciation expense of $26,667 is added to five-twelfths of the second full year's annual depreciation expense of $21,333. This two-step calculation continues until the truck's final year of use, at which time depreciation expense is calculated by multiplying the last full year's annual depreciation expense of $5,333 by seven-twelfths.

Sum-of-the-Years'-Digits Depreciation

	Portion of Year × SYD Fraction × Depreciable Cost	Annual Depreciation Expense	Accumulated Depreciation	Net Book Value
Cost				$90,000
Year 1 (5 mo.)	$5/12 \times 5/15 \times \$80,000$	$ 11,111	$ 11,111	78,889
Year 2	$7/12 \times 5/15 \times 80,000$ $+ 5/12 \times 4/15 \times 80,000$	24,445	35,556	54,444
Year 3	$7/12 \times 4/15 \times 80,000$ $+ 5/12 \times 3/15 \times 80,000$	19,111	54,667	35,333
Year 4	$7/12 \times 3/15 \times 80,000$ $+ 5/12 \times 2/15 \times 80,000$	13,778	68,445	21,555
Year 5	$7/12 \times 2/15 \times 80,000$ $+ 5/12 \times 1/15 \times 80,000$	8,444	76,889	13,111
Year 6 (7 mo.)	$7/12 \times 1/15 \times 80,000$	3,111	80,000	10,000

Revising depreciation estimates. Depreciation expense calculations depend upon estimates of an asset's useful life and expected salvage value. As time passes, a number of factors may cause these estimates to change. For example, after recording three years of depreciation expense on the truck, suppose the company decides the truck should be useful until it is seven rather than five years old and that its salvage value will be $14,000 instead of $10,000. Prior financial statements are not changed when useful life or salvage value estimates change, but subsequent depreciation expense calculations must be based upon the new estimates of the truck's useful life and depreciable cost.

Under the straight-line method, depreciation expense for years four through seven is calculated according to the equation below.

Revising Straight-Line Depreciation

$$\frac{\text{Net Book Value} - \text{New Salvage Value}}{\text{New Useful Life in Years}} = \begin{array}{c}\text{New Annual Depreciation} \\ \text{Expense}\end{array}$$

Assume that the company purchased the truck at the beginning of an annual accounting period. The table on page 180 shows how depreciation expense was calculated during the truck's first three years of use. The truck's net book value of $42,000 at the end of year three is reduced by the new, $14,000 estimate of salvage value to produce a revised depreciable cost of $28,000. The revised depreciable cost is divided by the four years now estimated to remain in the truck's useful life, yielding annual depreciation expense of $7,000.

$$\frac{\$42,000 - \$14,000}{4} = \$7,000$$

Similar revisions are made for each of the other depreciation methods. The asset's net book value when the revision is made along with new estimates of salvage value and useful life—measured in years or units—are used to calculate depreciation expense in subsequent years.

Depreciation for income tax purposes. In the United States, companies frequently use one depreciation method for financial reporting purposes and a different method for income tax purposes. Tax laws are complex and tend to change, at least slightly, from year to year. Therefore, this book does not attempt to explain specific income tax depreciation methods, but it is important to understand why most companies choose different income tax and financial reporting depreciation methods.

For financial reporting purposes, companies often select a depreciation method that apportions an asset's depreciable cost to expense in accordance with the matching principle. For income tax purposes, companies usually select a depreciation method that reduces or postpones taxable income and, therefore, tax payments. In the United States, straight-line depreciation is the method companies most frequently use for financial reporting purposes, and a special type of accelerated depreciation designed for income tax returns is the method they most frequently use for income tax purposes.

Repairs and Improvements

Expenses relating to depreciable assets fall into two broad categories: ordinary expenditures and capital expenditures. **Ordinary expenditures** include normal repairs, maintenance, and upkeep. The costs associated with these items are considered normal operating expenses, and they are recorded by debiting expense accounts and crediting cash or another appropriate account. **Capital expenditures** increase an asset's usefulness or service life, and they are recognized by increasing the asset's net book value.

There are two ways to increase an asset's net book value: the asset account can be debited, thus increasing the recognized cost of the asset, or the asset's corresponding accumulated depreciation account can be debited, thus decreasing the amount of depreciation previously allocated to the asset. If the capital expenditure serves primarily to increase the asset's usefulness or value, the asset account should be debited. On the other hand, if the capital expenditure serves primarily to increase the asset's useful life or salvage value, the accumulated depreciation account should be debited. Such judgments are not always clear cut, and discussions about the best way to record capital expenditures are usually covered in more advanced accounting courses. Nevertheless, you should be prepared to see capital expenditures recorded in either the asset account or the asset's accumulated depreciation account, and you should recognize that the effect on the asset's net book value is the same either way. Consider how a $10,000 capital expenditure changes the truck's net book value.

	Before Capital Expenditure	After $10,000 Capital Expenditure	
		Asset Account Debited	Accumulated Depreciation Debited
Cost	$90,000	100,000	90,000
Accumulated Depreciation	(64,000)	(64,000)	(54,000)
Net Book Value	$26,000	36,000	36,000

When capital expenditures are made, the revised net book value must be used to calculate depreciation expense in subsequent accounting periods.

The Disposition of Depreciable Assets

Depreciable assets are disposed of by retiring, selling, or exchanging them. When a depreciable asset is disposed of, an entry is made to recognize any unrecorded depreciation expense up to the date of the disposition, and then the asset's cost and accumulated depreciation are removed from the respective general ledger accounts. Any recognized losses or gains associated with the disposition are recorded in a separate account and appear in the portion of the income statement named *other income/(expense), net*.

Music World
Partial Income Statement
For the Year Ended June 30, 20X3

Operating Income		
Other Income/(Expense), Net		245,500
Interest Income	$ 7,500	
Gain on Sale of Equipment	1,500	
Interest Expense	(18,000)	
Other Income/(Expense), Net		(9,000)
Net Income		$ 236,500

Retirement of depreciable assets. Retirement occurs when a depreciable asset is taken out of service and no salvage value is received for the asset. In addition to removing the asset's cost and accumulated depreciation from the books, the asset's net book value, if it has any, is written off as a loss.

Suppose the $90,000 truck reaches the end of its useful life with a net book value of $10,000, but the truck is in such poor condition that a salvage yard simply agrees to haul it away for free. The entry to record the truck's retirement debits accumulated depreciation–vehicles for $80,000, debits loss on retirement of vehicles for $10,000, and credits vehicles for $90,000. The loss is considered an expense and decreases net income.

General Journal				GJ451
Date	Account Title and Description	Ref.	Debit	Credit
20X4				
May 31	Accumulated Depreciation–Vehicles	156	80,000	
	Loss on Retirement of Vehicles	590	10,000	
	Vehicles	155		90,000
	Retirement of truck			

A gain never occurs when an asset is retired. If the entire cost of an asset has been depreciated before it is retired, however, there is no loss. For example, if the company using the truck had expected no salvage value and, therefore, had allocated $90,000 in depreciation expense to the truck before its retirement, the disposition would be recorded simply by debiting accumulated depreciation–vehicles for $90,000 and crediting vehicles for $90,000.

General Journal				GJ451
Date	Account Title and Description	Ref.	Debit	Credit
20X4				
May 31	Accumulated Depreciation–Vehicles	156	90,000	
	Vehicles	155		90,000
	Retirement of truck			

Sale of depreciable assets. If an asset is sold for cash, the amount of cash received is compared to the asset's net book value to determine whether a gain or loss has occurred. Suppose the truck sells for $7,000 when its net book value is $10,000, resulting in a loss of $3,000. The sale is recorded by debiting accumulated depreciation–vehicles for $80,000, debiting cash for $7,000, debiting loss on sale of vehicles for $3,000, and crediting vehicles for $90,000.

	General Journal			GJ451
Date	Account Title and Description	Ref.	Debit	Credit
20X4				
May 31	Accumulated Depreciation–Vehicles	156	80,000	
	Cash	100	7,000	
	Loss on Sale of Vehicles	591	3,000	
	Vehicles	155		90,000
	Sale of truck			

If the truck sells for $15,000 when its net book value is $10,000, a gain of $5,000 occurs. The sale is recorded by debiting accumulated depreciation–vehicles for $80,000, debiting cash for $15,000, crediting vehicles for $90,000, and crediting gain on sale of vehicles for $5,000.

	General Journal			GJ451
Date	Account Title and Description	Ref.	Debit	Credit
20X4				
May 31	Accumulated Depreciation–Vehicles	156	80,000	
	Cash	100	15,000	
	Vehicles	155		90,000
	Gain on Sale of Vehicles	491		5,000
	Sale of truck			

Exchange of depreciable assets. Certain types of assets, particularly vehicles and large pieces of equipment, are frequently exchanged for other tangible assets. For example, an old vehicle and a negotiated amount of cash may be exchanged for a new vehicle.

There are two types of exchanges: similar exchanges and dissimilar exchanges. A **similar exchange** involves the exchange of one asset for another asset that performs the same type of function. Trading in an old delivery truck to purchase a new delivery truck is an example of a similar exchange. A **dissimilar exchange,** which is less common than a similar exchange, involves the exchange of one asset for another asset that performs a different function. Trading in an old truck for a forklift is an example of a dissimilar exchange.

Suppose a $90,000 delivery truck with a net book value of $10,000 is exchanged for a new delivery truck. The company receives a $6,000 trade-in allowance on the old truck and pays an additional $95,000 for the new truck, so a loss on exchange of $4,000 must be recognized.

Cost of Truck Traded In	$90,000
Less: Accumulated Depreciation	(80,000)
Net Book Value	10,000
Trade-in Value	(6,000)
Loss on Exchange	$ 4,000

The cost of the new truck is $101,000 ($95,000 cash + $6,000 trade-in allowance). Therefore, the exchange is recorded by debiting vehicles for $101,000 (to record the new truck's cost), debiting accumulated depreciation–vehicles for $80,000 (to remove the old truck's accumulated depreciation from the books), debiting loss on exchange of vehicles for $4,000, crediting vehicles for $90,000 (to remove the old truck from the books), and crediting cash for $95,000.

General Journal   GJ451

Date	Account Title and Description	Ref.	Debit	Credit
20X4				
May 31	Vehicles	155	101,000	
	Accumulated Depreciation – Vehicles	156	80,000	
	Loss on Exchange of Vehicles	592	4,000	
	Vehicles	155		90,000
	Cash	100		95,000
	Exchange old truck for new truck			

If the company exchanges its used truck for a forklift, receives a $6,000 trade-in allowance, and pays $20,000 for the forklift, the loss on exchange is still $4,000. Assuming the company uses a separate account to record the cost of forklifts, the journal entry to record this dissimilar exchange debits forklifts for $26,000, debits accumulated depreciation–vehicles for $80,000, debits loss on exchange of vehicles for $4,000, credits vehicles for $90,000, and credits cash for $20,000.

General Journal				GJ451
Date	Account Title and Description	Ref.	Debit	Credit
20X4				
May 31	Forklifts	175	26,000	
	Accumulated Depreciation–Vehicles	156	80,000	
	Loss on Exchange of Vehicles	592	4,000	
	Vehicles	155		90,000
	Cash	100		20,000
	Exchange old truck for new forklift			

If the company receives a $12,000 trade-in allowance, a gain of $2,000 occurs.

Cost of Truck Traded In	$90,000
Less: Accumulated Depreciation	(80,000)
Net Book Value	10,000
Trade-in Value	(12,000)
Gain on Exchange	($ 2,000)

Gains on similar exchanges are handled differently from gains on dissimilar exchanges. On a similar exchange, gains are deferred and reduce the cost of the new asset. For example, after receiving a $12,000 trade-in allowance on a delivery truck with a net book value of $10,000 and paying $89,000 in cash for a new delivery truck, the company records the cost of the new truck at $99,000 instead of $101,000. The $99,000 cost of the new truck equals the $12,000 trade-in allowance plus the $89,000 cash payment minus the $2,000 gain. Since the $12,000 trade-in allowance minus the $2,000 gain equals the old truck's net book value of $10,000, however, it is easier to think of the $99,000 cost as being equal to the old truck's net book value of $10,000 plus the $89,000 paid in cash. To record this exchange, the company debits vehicles for $99,000 (to record the new truck's recognized cost), debits accumulated depreciation–vehicles for $80,000 (to remove the old truck's accumulated depreciation from the books), credits vehicles for $90,000 (to remove the old truck from the books), and credits cash for $89,000.

General Journal — GJ451

Date	Account Title and Description	Ref.	Debit	Credit
20X4				
May 31	Vehicles	155	99,000	
	Accumulated Depreciation–Vehicles	156	80,000	
	Vehicles	155		90,000
	Cash	100		89,000
	Exchange old truck for new truck			

Gains on dissimilar exchanges are recognized when the transaction occurs. After receiving a $12,000 trade-in allowance on a truck with a $10,000 net book value and paying $14,000 in cash for a forklift, the company debits forklifts for $26,000, debits accumulated depreciation–vehicles for $80,000, credits vehicles for $90,000, credits cash for $14,000, and credits gain on exchange of vehicles for $2,000.

General Journal — GJ451

Date	Account Title and Description	Ref.	Debit	Credit
20X4				
May 31	Forklifts	175	26,000	
	Accumulated Depreciation–Vehicles	156	80,000	
	Vehicles	155		90,000
	Cash	100		14,000
	Gain on Exchange of Vehicles	492		2,000
	Exchange old truck for new forklift			

Natural Resources

Timber, fossil fuels, mineral deposits, and other natural resources are different from depreciable assets because they are physically extracted during company operations and they are replaceable only through natural processes.

Cost of natural resources. The cost of natural resources includes all costs necessary to acquire the resource and prepare it for extraction. If the property must be restored after the natural resources are removed, the restoration costs are also considered to be part of the cost.

Companies that search for new natural resources determine cost using one of two approaches: the successful-efforts approach or the full-cost approach. Under the **successful-efforts approach,** exploration costs are considered part of the cost of natural resources only when a productive natural resource is found. Unsuccessful exploration costs are treated as expenses in the period during which they occur. Under the **full-cost approach,** all exploration costs are included in the cost of natural resources. The approach that a company selects should be disclosed in the notes that accompany the financial statements.

Depletion. Depletion is the process of allocating the depletable cost of natural resources to expense as individual units of the resource are extracted. **Depletable cost** equals the total cost of natural resources less any salvage value remaining after the company finishes extracting them. Depletion expense is generally calculated using the units-of-activity method. Under this method, a per-unit cost of depletion is found by dividing the depletable cost by the estimated number of units the resource contains. The per-unit cost times the actual number of units extracted and sold in one year equals the amount of depletion expense recorded for the asset during that year.

Calculating Units-of-Activity Depletion

$$\frac{\text{Depletable Cost}}{\text{Units of Resource}} = \text{Per-Unit Depletion}$$

$$\text{Per-Unit Depletion} \times \text{Units During Year} = \text{Annual Depletion Expense}$$

Suppose a company pays $50,000,000 for an existing gold mine estimated to contain 1,000,000 ounces of gold. The mine has no salvage value, so the depletable cost of $50,000,000 is divided by 1,000,000 ounces to calculate a per-unit depletion cost of $50 per ounce. If the company extracts and then sells 100,000 ounces of gold during the year, depletion expense equals $5,000,000.

Calculating Units-of-Activity Depletion

$$\frac{\$50,000,000}{1,000,000 \text{ ounces}} = \$50 \text{ per ounce}$$

$$\$50 \text{ per ounce} \times 100,000 \text{ ounces} = \$5,000,000$$

One way to record depletion expense of $5,000,000 is to debit depletion expense for $5,000,000 and credit accumulated depletion–mine for $5,000,000.

General Journal   GJ98

Date	Account Title and Description	Ref.	Debit	Credit
20X9				
Dec. 31	Depletion Expense	566	5,000,000	
	Accumulated Depletion–Mine	166		5,000,000
	Depletion of 100,000 ounces			

Instead of using a contra-asset account to record accumulated depletion, companies may also decrease the balance of natural resources directly. Therefore, depletion expense of $5,000,000 might be recorded by debiting depletion expense for $5,000,000 and crediting the gold mine for $5,000,000.

General Journal   GJ98

Date	Account Title and Description	Ref.	Debit	Credit
20X9				
Dec. 31	Depletion Expense	566	5,000,000	
	Mine	165		5,000,000
	Depletion of 100,000 ounces			

Intangible Assets

Intangible assets include patents, copyrights, trademarks, trade names, franchise licenses, government licenses, goodwill, and other items that lack physical substance but provide long-term benefits to the company. Companies account for intangible assets much as they account for depreciable assets and natural resources. The cost of intangible assets is systematically allocated to expense during the asset's useful life or legal life, whichever is shorter, and this life is never allowed to exceed forty years. The process of allocating the cost of intangible assets to expense is called amortization, and companies almost always use the straight-line method to amortize intangible assets.

Patents. Patents provide exclusive rights to produce or sell new inventions. When a patent is purchased from another company, the cost of the patent is the purchase price. If a company invents a new product and receives a patent for it, the cost includes only registration, documentation, and legal fees associated with acquiring the patent and defending it against unlawful use by other companies. **Research and development costs,** which are spent to improve existing products or create new ones, are never included in the cost of a patent; such costs are recorded as operating expenses when they are incurred because of the uncertainty surrounding the benefits they will provide.

The legal life of a patent is seventeen years, which often exceeds the patent's useful life. Suppose a company buys an existing, five-year-old patent for $100,000. The patent's remaining legal life is twelve years. If the company believes the patent's remaining useful life is only ten years, they use the straight-line method to calculate that $10,000 ($100,000 ÷ 10 = $10,000) must be recorded as amortization expense each year.

One way to record amortization expense of $10,000 is to debit amortization expense for $10,000 and credit accumulated amortization–patent for $10,000.

General Journal				GJ848
Date	Account Title and Description	Ref.	Debit	Credit
20X6				
Dec. 31	Amortization Expense	576	10,000	
	Accumulated Amortization–Patent	176		10,000
	Annual amortization of patent			

Instead of using a contra-asset account to record accumulated amortization, most companies decrease the balance of the intangible asset directly. In such cases, amortization expense of $10,000 is recorded by debiting amortization expense for $10,000 and crediting the patent for $10,000.

General Journal				GJ848
Date	Account Title and Description	Ref.	Debit	Credit
20X6				
Dec. 31	Amortization Expense	576	10,000	
	Patent	175		10,000
	Annual amortization of patent			

A similar entry would be made to record amortization expense for each type of intangible asset. The entry would include a debit to amortization expense and a credit to the accumulated amortization or intangible asset account.

Copyrights. Companies amortize a variety of intangible assets, depending on the nature of the business. **Copyrights** provide their owner with the exclusive right to reproduce and sell artistic works, such as books, songs, or movies. The cost of copyrights includes a nominal registration fee and any expenditures associated with defending the copyright. If a copyright is purchased, the purchase price determines the amortizable cost. Although the legal life of a copyright is extensive, copyrights are often fully amortized within a relatively short period of time. The amortizable life of a copyright, like other intangible assets, may never exceed forty years.

Trademarks and trade names. **Trademarks** and **trade names** include corporate logos, advertising jingles, and product names that have been registered with the government and serve to identify specific companies and products. All expenditures associated with securing and defending trademarks and trade names are amortizable.

Franchise licenses. The purchaser of a **franchise license** receives the right to sell certain products or services and to use certain trademarks or trade names. These rights are valuable because they provide the purchaser with immediate customer recognition. Many fast-food restaurants, hotels, gas stations, and automobile dealerships are owned by individuals who have paid a company for a franchise license. The cost of a franchise license is amortized over its useful life, often its contractual life, which is not to exceed forty years.

Government licenses. The purchaser of a **government license** receives the right to engage in regulated business activities. For example, government licenses are required to broadcast on specific frequencies and to transport certain materials. The cost of government licenses is amortizable in the same way as franchise licenses.

Goodwill. **Goodwill** equals the amount paid to acquire a company in excess of its net assets at fair market value. The excess payment may result from the value of the company's reputation, location, customer list, management team, or other intangible factors. Goodwill may be recorded only after the purchase of a company occurs because such a transaction provides an objective measure of goodwill as recognized by the purchaser. The value of goodwill is calculated by first subtracting the purchased company's liabilities from the fair market value (not the net book value) of its assets and then subtracting this result from the purchase price of the company.

Fair Market Value of Assets
− Liabilities
= Net Assets at Fair Market Value

Purchase Price of Company
− Net Assets at Fair Market Value
= Goodwill

Suppose Yard Apes, Inc., purchases the Greener Landscape Group for $50,000. When the purchase takes place, the Greener Landscape Group has assets with a fair market value of $45,000 and liabilities of $15,000, so the company would seem to be worth only $30,000.

The Greener Landscape Group
Fair Market Value of Assets and Liabilities
July 31, 20X5

Assets		Liabilities	
Cash	$ 6,000	Accounts Payable	$ 3,000
Accounts Receivable	4,000	Wages Payable	1,000
Supplies	1,000	Unearned Revenue	2,000
Prepaid Insurance	2,000	Notes Payable	9,000
Equipment	12,000	Total Liabilities	$15,000
Vehicles	20,000		
Total Assets	$45,000		

Since Yard Apes, Inc., is willing to pay $50,000, they must recognize that the Greener Landscape Group's value includes $20,000 in goodwill. Yard Apes, Inc., makes the entry shown below to record the purchase of the Greener Landscape Group.

General Journal				GJ97
Date	Account Title and Description	Ref.	Debit	Credit
20X5				
July 31	Cash	100	6,000	
	Accounts Receivable	110	4,000	
	Supplies	140	1,000	
	Prepaid Insurance	145	2,000	
	Equipment	150	12,000	
	Vehicles	155	20,000	
	Goodwill	190	20,000	
	Accounts Payable	200		3,000
	Wages Payable	210		1,000
	Unearned Revenue	250		2,000
	Notes Payable	280		9,000
	Cash	100		50,000
	Purchase Greener Landscape Group for $50,000 in cash			

Yard Apes, Inc., believes the useful life of the goodwill is five years. Using the straight-line method, Yard Apes, Inc., calculates that $4,000 in goodwill must be amortized each year ($20,000 \div 5 = $4,000). To record a full year's amortization expense, they debit amortization expense for $4,000 and credit goodwill for $4,000.

General Journal				GJ164
Date	Account Title and Description	Ref.	Debit	Credit
20X6				
July 31	Amortization Expense	576	4,000	
	Goodwill	190		4,000
	Annual amortization of goodwill